Chez HUBERT
25 rue de l'Hirondelle
UNIVERSITÉ
faculté russe
(2e et 4e vendredi)
le 12 mai 1922
à 21.00 heures

Place St.Michel — VIe — Ve de la Hachette — St.André des Arts — St.Séverin — boul St.Michel — Hautefeuille

41°

ILIAzDE ИЛІАзДА
l'éloge de ILIA элога ИЛЬИ
ZDANÉVITCH ЗДАНЕВИЧА
nommé l'ANGE прозваннаго АНГЕЛОМ
sur lui même о самом себе

crétin
lâche бездарном хамѣ трусѣ предателе
traître идіотѣ подлецѣ и царьгрязной бляхе
fripouille
assassin суть:на дне рожденія·тріумфально зачат:
détrousseur ует трех зубов·слишком кудри·. рак
crapule ом пятится·пороки и пророки·де нуар
chenapan и бель етаж·кои что о бреках·целом
удрие·бискровнае убійство и бѣвоный
язык·тайны и болезни·путешестви
е в албанію·рекорд нѣжности·au,сися,
осел за человека и наоборот·скульптурныя занятія
половинка бзыпызы·облиэ кремер·почти апас
сіоната·сошествіе святаго запредухія·орфей
у труперд·недопустимыя возможности·в детской

билеты у Поволоцкаго, Родштейна, в Зеленой палочкѣ, Librairie Universelle, The Kittymуада

Poster for Ilya Zdanevich's lecture 'Iliazda'

Ilya Zdanevich — Iliazd
Iliazda at the Birthday Party
Autobiographical Lecture, 1922

bie bao series   militant zaum investigations volume 2

Introduction

Ilya Zdanevich gave the *Iliazda* lecture on May 12th 1922 in the Parisian cabaret theatre *Le Caveau de la Bolée*, which had been an old haunt for anarchists, students, hooligans, prostitutes and poets since the days of Baudelaire.[1] Ever since he arrived from Tbilisi, via Istanbul, Zdanevich had established himself in the avant-garde art world of Paris as an impressive orator. Prior to *Iliazda*, he gave lectures about 'The New School in Russian Poetry' on November 27th 1921, '*Le degré 41 sinapisé*' on February 22nd 1922, 'House on Shit' on April 16th 1922, and 'Poetry after Bath' on April 28th 1922. All of these lectures were part of the curriculum of the University of the Forty-first Degree [41°], a new artistic-pedagogic platform he was establishing from the ashes of revolutionary Russian Futurism in the land of war-torn European Dada.[2] The 41° organisation in Paris was projected to be "a society for the building and exploitation of the world's political ideas," bridging contemporary ideas from New York to Samarkand, Paris to Tehran, Berlin to Moscow, London to Tbilisi.[3] Zaum was declared as the language of this new internationalism.

In the poster Zdanevich designed especially for the *Iliazda* lecture – using a cut and paste technique that makes the image look as if refracted – the talk is announced in French and Russian, as a "eulogy of Ilya Zdanevich, named the angel by himself." The poster also described Zdanevich as "a mediocre boor, a coward, a traitor, an idiot, a scoundrel, and a dirty tsar flea" in Russian, and "a cretin, sluggard, traitor, assassin, robber, scoundrel, shithead" in French. Zdanevich in this lecture introduced himself to a Parisian audience and discussed the "record of tenderness, journey to Albania, ai sisya, bloodless murder and yvonne [yt] language," which were the names for some of artistic moments he had experienced earlier in St. Petersburg and Tbilisi.

Iliazda was "a clownish autobiography, following the model of the Iliada, introducing real and semi-legendary incidents. Along with an autobiography full of self-admiration, in this lecture Zdanevich gives an interpretation of his zaum dramas inspired by Freudianism, outlines a funny image of the Russian microcosm in Montparnasse, and once again specifies his place and direction on the chessboard of Russian poetry (he had already devoted the first four lectures to this topic)."[4] A paronomasia he used for this occasion was destined to have a great future – "Iliazda" was a wordplay combining the name Ilya Zdanevich with Iliada. In French, he first transcribed his pseudonym with a feminine ending (Iliazde), hinting at the transsexual motifs of his autobiography, but soon he finally chose the spelling Iliazd, which he used as a name for the rest of his life.[5]

In June 1922, soon after this lecture, Zdanevich began to write a new version of it, which he sought to expand into a whole book. *Iliazda* as a book was never finished, but most of his writings continued to be semi-autobiographical.[6] On the back of the existing

                    Introduction

short manuscript of the planned book, which Régis
Gayraud mentions, there is a small note dividing his
life into three periods, or phases:

1. Girl, twelve years. 0–12 years (1894–1906).
2. Charlatan, twelve years (1906–1918).
3. *Dunkeeness* years (1918–1922).[7]

At the time of writing his autobiography, Zdanevich,
under the influence of Igor Terentiev, was interested
in applying Freud's theories into his zaum practice,
which is evident from the importance he gave
to chance and aleatoriness, but as well as in the
prevalence of sexual references. Rewriting his
childhood from a sexually queer perspective is
clearly a reference to psychoanalytical concept of
"polymorphous perversity", intending to challenge
the very foundation of Western bourgeois moralism,
a project that united Freud and transgressive artists
like Zdanevich.

The charlatan years of Zdanevich, as he calls
this period, lasted until 1918 and were artistically
the most active phase; six years of that period were
completely immersed in Futurist activities. In 1911
Zdanevich translated Italian Futurist manifestos
into Russian and began to correspond with Filippo
Marinetti. In 1912 he read these Futurist manifestos
at the Troitsky Theatre in St. Petersburg. In 1912–13,
he discovered Niko Pirosmani, an outsider artist
from Tbilisi, and enveloped him into the Futurist
constellation. In 1913, he sermonised his own

version of Futurism under the name *Everythingism*, incorporating every different form from all existing epochs and civilizations. That same year he published a book on Natalia Goncharova and Mikhail Larionov under the pseudonym Eli Eganbyuri. Influenced by the work of Velimir Khlebnikov and Alexei Kruchenykh, he wrote *gaRoland*, his first sound poem. In 1916 his involvement with the Futurist group Bloodless Murder began, and influenced by the special issue of their journal dedicated to Albania, he wrote and performed *Yanko, King of Albania*, his first zaum drama.

During this period, Zdanevich also wrote reportages critical of imperialist wars and Russian policies towards minorities for the constitutional-democratic newspaper *Rech*. After the February Revolution in 1917 Zdanevich was involved in the Federation of Free Arts, energetically organising an opposition against the proposal to appoint a bourgeois art critic as the Minister of Culture in the newly formed democratic country. The October Revolution caught him in the Caucasus. In 1918, he established the Futurist Syndicate in Tbilisi.[8]

The third phase of his artistic biography, from 1918 to 1922, were years of the *dunkeeness* period that made him a representative of "the extreme wing of the Russian avant-garde."[9] A large portion of this militant period was set in Tbilisi, where Zdanevich wrote and designed four out of five of his zaum dramas, or *dras*, as he was calling them, where donkeys played an important role: *Yanko, King of Albania*; *Donkey for Rent*; *Easter Eyeland*; and

As if Zga. The fifth and the final of these dramas,
Ledentu as Beacon, which he dedicated to his
Futurist friend Mikhail Le Dentu, was published in
Paris in 1923. As Vladimir Markov argued, *dras* are
the "most consistent and large-scale use of zaum in
Russian Futurist literature," the project which made
Ilya Zdanevich into a "classicist of zaum."[10] In 1922,
when Zdanevich gave the autobiographical *Iliazda*
lecture, his main occupation was to compose a
scientific methodology from zaum experiments that
could exploit "extremely rich and unexplored areas
of language."[11] Lectures he read in Paris from 1921
to 1923, like *Le degré 41 sinapisé*, aimed at uniting
all avant-garde discoveries into one school. He was
"genuinely persuasive"[12] in giving a scientific pretext
to 'beyond-sense' inquiries. Zdanevich's lectures
were carefully elaborated "cold insights."[13]

In the beginning of the twenties, there was hardly
a room for cold insights in Paris. Dadaists, with whom
Zdanevich aligned, were "approaching a crisis to
which there was no solution."[14] Picabia was against
Tzara, Ribemont-Dessaignes against Picabia, Tzara
against Breton, Breton against Picabia, and so on – in
this whirlpool of "confusion" where Zdanevich found
himself, a scientific approach to the avant-garde did
not help much. Despite all this mess, Zdanevich and
other Russian avant-garde artists in Paris joined in
the ongoing turmoil. At the time of the *Iliazda* lecture,
Zdanevich sided with Tristan Tzara, and he designed
the cover of the only issue of the newspaper *Le Cœur
à Barbe* [The Bearded Heart], published by Tzara in

April 1922, as a response to the attack launched by
Breton.[15] In the infamous 1923 soirée '*Le Cœur à Barbe*',
which violently split Dadaists and future Surrealists,
Zdanevich, a supporter of Tzara, read his phonetic
[zaum] poems to no avail.[16] This, for Zdanevich, was the
end of the anarchist *dunkeeness* period .[17]

Together with other Russian avant-garde
poets close to Dadaism, like Sergey Sharshun,
Boris Poplavsky, and Sergei Romov, Zdanevich
was conceiving a parallel organisation, something
similar to the Left Front of the Arts [*Levy Front
Iskusstv,* LEF]. He was associated with the group
Udar [Strike], which arranged Mayakovsky's visit to
Paris in November 1922. Upon that visit they decided
to initiate a platform *Cherez* [Through, Across],
which would be the Paris contingent of the LEF,
strengthening the relationship between French and
Soviet avant-garde artists.[18] As Leonid Livak, in his
article on Russian avant-garde milieu in Paris writes,
one of the important traits in the Dadaist groups
around Zdanevich was "the absence of anti-Soviet
attitudes among the organisers and members."[19]
This was an important distinction, as during these
years, in fact up until 1924, France did not have
diplomatic relations with the Soviet Union, and Paris
was a stronghold for all sorts of White émigrés
fleeing Russia. As Jean Giraudoux wrote, during these
years in Parisian restaurants "the bread was served
by Pushkin's great nephew and the grand-daughters
of Ivan the Terrible passed the salt."[20] As a contrats,
among the editors of the Russian Dadaists journal

Introduction

Udar [Strike, 1922–23] were Anatoly Lunacharsky,
Ilya Ehrenburg, and other eminent Soviets.[21]

Iliazd's letter to Ardengo Soffici from 1964,
often referred to as '50 years of Futurism', is an
important document for understanding this history.
It is an unapologetic defence of the independence
of avant-garde art, but also an unambiguous critique
of the right-wing revisionism that occurred under
the pretence of defending apolitical positions in
contemporary art. In his letter to Soffici, Iliazd
is unambiguously clear about his leftist political
commitments. It is true, as Régis Gayraud writes in
the introduction to the Iliazd-Soffici correspondence,
that between 1924 to 1926, Iliazd worked in the Soviet
embassy in Paris, which was a fact he himself did not
hide. Nevertheless, it is misleading to claim that there
was some indispensable link between Futurism and
power, and that "Futurism, whether Italian or Russian,
has been linked with dictatorial powers."[22] Iliazd, in
his letter to Soffici, who was a Fascist supporter of
Mussolini in the thirties and forties, draws the line of
demarcation between Russian and Italian Futurism,
especially through its political conjuncture, precisely
through war and revolution. Most of the Russian
Futurists were in opposition to the imperialist wars of
the Russian Empire and most of them embraced the
October Revolution. They were unlike the Western
Futurists, who represented a movement that was
"like a plant which came to bud too early; remained
frozen and withered [...] caught out by a political frost
of militarism and patriotism."[23]

On the same day when Zdanevich read his
paper 'Iliazda' in Paris, May 12th 1922, Leon Trotsky
in Moscow read his report 'From the Executive
Committee of The Communist International to the
Central Committee of the French Communist Party.'
Trotsky and other Soviet leaders during the first five
years of activities of the Communist International
(1919–1924) had given particular attention to France.
Trotsky's critique was against the bourgeois elements
in the French Communist Party and he was calling
for a "cleansing, consolidating and strengthening
the party's principles,"[24] from "intimate ties with
the League for the Defence of the Rights of Man
and Citizen, freemasonry and the bourgeoisie
press."[25] This militant energy of cultural and political
emancipation, which was unleashed with the October
Revolution, did not spare even the avant-garde of
Paris.[26] Iliazd's letter to Soffici discerns some of
these links and speculates on its possible future
expressions.

After the Dadaist fiasco and the Stalinist
backlash, in the mid-twenties Zdanevich departed
both from Tzara's soirées and *Udar's* activities.[27]
The plans made with the University of the 41 Degree
in Paris came to nothing. From then on, design and
typography became a new direction in Zdanevich's
skills for organising. First in collaborations with Sonya
Delaunay, and later with his job at Coco Chanel, as
a designer and manager, Iliazd's 'cold insights', for a
period of time became part of the fashion industry.[28]
He recommenced his activities as designer in 1940

with a series of beautifully produced artist books, which were considered a revolution in design and typography.[29] These publications changed the ways we engage with books, often by extending their artistic content with the advanced technical possibilities of printing. With Iliazd, the artists' books entered a new life, which continues to live on today. As Johanna Drucker has succinctly written, "he began to *think* and *write* with an understanding of letterpress."[30] This technique was also made possible through the leftist networks. Starting with *lidantYU fAram* [Ledentu as Beacon] in 1923, Iliazd published almost all his books at l'Imprimerie Union, a printing and typographic workshop set up on Lenin's request by two Bolsheviks in exile in Paris in 1909.[31]

Introduction

1 'Iliazda: Na Dne Rozhdeniya', in Ilya Zdanevich, *Dom na Govne: doklady i vystupleniya v Parizhe i Berline, 1921–1926* [House on Shit: reports and speeches in Paris and Berlin, 1921–1926], edited by Sergey Kudriavtsev, with commentaries by Régis Gayraud, and Kudriavtsev, Hylea, Moscow, 2021, pp. 570–571.

2 "41 Degree was the latitude of some of the greatest cities of light – Madrid, Napoli, Istanbul, Peking, New York." Raimond Cogniat, 'L'Université du degré 41. Un laboratoire de poesie', Comoedia, 4.12. 1921. Quote taken from the Russian translation in *Literaturnyi avangard russkogo Parizha : 1920-1926, Istoriia, khronika, antologiia, dokumenty*, edited by Leonid Livak and Andrei Ustinov, OGI, Moscow, 2014, p. 815.

3 Quoted from a document in Zdanevich Archives in Françoise Le Gris-Bergmann, 'Iliazd and the Constellation of His Oeuvre', *Iliazd and the illustrated Book*, edited by Maura Walsh, The Museum of Modern Art, New York, 1987, p. 44.

4 Régis Gayraud, 'Doklad Iliji Zdanevica "Iliazda" [Ilya Zdanevich's Lecture 'Iliazda'],' *Poeziya i Zhivopis: Sbornik trudov pamyati N. I. Khardzhieva*, Yazyki Russkoi Kul'tury, Moscow, 2000, p. 518.

5 Gayraud, 'Doklad Iliji Zdanevica', p. 520. "The name also recalled the Zoroastrian god Ahura-Mazda and evoked the Russian words for 'star' (zvezda) and 'cunt' (pizda). It is also a simple assertion in French of his existence: Il y a Zda (his intimate friends called him 'Zda')." Thomas Kitson, 'Introduction to *Rapture*: The Golden Excrement of the Avant-Garde', in *Iliazd, Rapture*, transl. by T. Kitson, Columbia University Press, 2017, p. 181.

6 Zdanevich's novel *Filosofiia* is, as Thomas Kitson argues, a "semi-autobiographical" work, presented as "a secret in motion." Kitson also adds that "Iliazd welcomed ceaseless metamorphoses, the cat's nine lives, continual rebirth here on earth, even after death." Thomas Kitson, 'Introduction to *Rapture*: The Golden Excrement of the Avant-Garde', p. xiix.

7 A two-page short version of 'Iliazda', was written in June 1922, and is mostly about his childhood. It was first published in *Poeziya i Zhivopis: Sbornik trudov pamyati N. I. Khardzhieva*, as a short addition to the 'Iliazda' lecture. In a new edited version, Gayraud and Kudriavtsev mention a brief note written by Zdanevich on the reverse side of the manuscript, "Write about yourself in the feminine noun." *Dom na Govne: doklady i vystupleniya v Parizhe i Berline*, p. 627.

8 For a sketchy biography of Zdanevich: Petr Kazarnovskii, 'Zdanevich, Ilia,' *Entsiklopediia russkogo avangarda: Izobrazitel'noe iskusstvo, arkhitektura*, Vol. I, Biografii A-K [Encyclopaedia of the Russian Avant-garde, Vol. 1: Biographies A-K], (Global Expert and Service Team, Moscow, 2014), p. 354. François Maire, 'Iliazd – Ilia Zdanevitch,' and 'Biographie du poète et éditeur Iliazd', both in *Dada po-russki*, edited by Kornelia Ičin, Belgrade University, 2013, pp. 5–20. For a more comprehensive and poetic biography, Johanna Drucker, *Iliazd: A Meta-Biography of a Modernist*, John Hopkins University Press, 2020.

9 Lucien Scheler, 'Le Magicien du Mont Caucase', *Bulletin du Bibliophile, No. 2*, 1974, p. 180. *dunkeeness*, or *dUnkeeness*, is adaptation of *aslaabliche*, which in literal translation would be "donkeyness."

10 Vladimir Markov, *Russian Futurism: A History*, University of California Press, 1968, p. 351, 357.

11 Quoted from a document in Zdanevich Archives in Françoise Le Gris-Bergmann, 'Iliazd and the Constellation of His Oeuvre', p. 44.

12 Markov, *Russian Futurism*, p. 357.

13 Zdanevich's own statement, taken from Janecek: "We left the realm of onomatopoeia for the realm of zaum, the world of abstraction, mental games and great, *cold insights*." Gerald Janecek, *Zaum: The Transrational Poetry of Russian Futurism*, San Diego State University Press, 1996, p. 285.

14 Hans Richter, *Dada: Art and Anti-Art*, Thames and Hudson, London, 1965, p. 186.

15 Margarita Tupitsyn, 'Putting Russia on the Dada Map', *Russian Dada, 1914–1924*, The MIT Press, 2018, p. 146.

16 Richter, *Dada: Art and Anti-Art*, pp. 188–190.

17 In 1923, after publishing *lidantYU fAram* [Ledentu as Beacon], his final *dra* book, Zdanevich wrote "I throw out this book, farewell youth, farewell zaum, farewell long path of acrobatics, of ambiguity, of cold logic, of everything, everything, everything." Unpublished text, quoted in Françoise Le Gris-Bergmann, 'Iliazd and the Constellation of His Oeuvre', p. 25.

18 Leonid Livak, *Geroicheskie vremena molodoi zarubezhnoi poezii* [Heroic times of young foreign poetry], in *Literaturnyi avangard russkogo Parizha*, pp. 72–75. Zdanevich's attachment to Mayakovsky was seen as a

Introduction

possibility in the artistic-political conjuncture of Paris. "The writer and literary critic André Garmain's lecture 'Ilia Zdanevich and Russian Surdadaism,' delivered on November 28th (a few days after Mayakovsky's departure), hints at recruiting the Russians into the surrealists' camp just as the competition between the two groups was heating up." Tupitsyn, 'Putting Russia on the Dada Map', p. 143.

19 Livak, 'Geroicheskie vremena molodoi zarubezhnoi poezii,' p. 16.

20 Quoted in Walter Benjamin, 'V.I. Lenin, Letters to Maxim Gorky, 1908–1913', translated by Esther Leslie, *Rab-Rab: Journal of Political and Formal Inquiries in Art, Volume 6*, Helsinki, 2021, unpaginated insert.

21 Between February 1922 and August 1923, four issues of *Udar* were published. Most of the texts were about French modern and contemporary artists. Only the chronicles section included news about Russian avant-garde artists living in Paris. The fourth and final issue published a detailed chronicle on *Cherez* and *Udar*, including news about Mayakovsky's visit and Zdanevich's lectures on zaum. The facsimile edition of all four issues were reprinted in *Literaturnyi avangard russkogo Parizha : 1920–1926*, pp. 887–990.

22 Régis Gayraud, 'Quand Iliazd écrit à Soffici : une histoire dans l'histoire', *Cahiers de la Méditerranée No. 90*, 2015, p. 7.

23 Nikolai Gorlov, "Futurism and Revolution [1924]", *The Futurists, The Formalists & The Marxist Critique*, edited by Chris Pike, Ink Links, London, 1979, p. 191. The Western Futurists were embracing "militarism and patriotism, which is to protect, to preserve, to re-establish, to place everything on its old footing," the values which the avant-garde was determined to demolish. Gorlov, "Futurism and Revolution [1924]", p. 188.

24 Leon Trotsky, 'From the ECCI to the Central Committee of the French Communist Party (May 12 1922)', *The First Five Years of the Communist International, Volume Two*, New Park Publications, London, 1974, p. 124.

25 Leon Trotsky, 'Resolution of the Fourth World Congress on the French Question (1 December 1922)', in *Theses, Resolutions and Manifestos of the First Four Congress of the Third International*, Pluto Press, London, 1982, pp. 351–353.

26 Zdanevich was never a member of the Communist Party, but neither was he an anti-communist, which he makes clear in his letter to Soffici. Zdanevich, at most, was

Introduction

a leftist fellow-traveller, standing resolutely against nationalism, imperialism and war. As he wrote in his semi-autobiography *Filosofiia*, "Iliazd had an external relationship with the adherents of Zimmerwald," which is to say, he had sympathies with the socialists who declared their opposition to war in Zimmerwald in 1916. Iliazd, 'Filosofiia [1930]', *Filosofiia futurista: Romany i zaumnye dramy*, Hilea, Moscow, 2008, p. 188.

27 "In 1928, Romov returned to the Soviet Union, where he disappeared in Stalin's purges in 1938. His essay 'From Dada to Surrealism' ('Ot dada k siurrealizmu,' *Vestnik inostrannoi literatury, no. 3*, 1929) is one of the most reliable primary sources." Victor Tupitsyn, 'Dada in Cyrillic', *Russian Dada, 1914–1924*, pp. 200–201. Romov's text is reprinted in *Literaturnyi avangard russkogo Parizha: 1920–1926*, pp. 851–886.

28 For balls such a "travesti transmental" [queer zaum], which Iliazd organized in 1923 in Paris, "gave rise to Sonia Delaunay's most accomplished costumes." Cécile Bargues, 'Sonia Delaunay, Tristan Tzara, Iliazd and others', *Sonia Delaunay*, Tate Publishing, London, 2015, p. 115. Iliazd designed shawls for Delaunay's firm, and worked as designer for Coco Chanel from 1927 to 1933.

29 This is a fact recognised by many, and affirmed by a statement of Louis Barnier, head of L'Imprimerie Union where Iliazd published most of his books, in his untitled essay in *Bulletin du Bibliophile, No. 2*, 1974, 129–146. Iliazd himself wrote about his revolutionary discovery in typography. "It is in this book [*La Maigre*, 1952] that I introduced for the first time the exclusive use of variable spacing between letters in order to balance and lighten the lines. This invention demonstrated the error committed by Renaissance artists in their quest for proportions of rounded letters as they studied each letter separately instead of envisioning the [typographical] whole." Quoted in Audrey Isselbacher, 'Iliazd and the Tradition of the 'Livre de Peintre'', *Iliazd and the illustrated Book*, p. 17. For an annotated bibliography of Iliazd's artists' books, François Chapon, 'Bibliographie descriptive des livres édités par Iliazd de 1940 à 1974', *Bulletin du Bibliophile, No. 2*, 1974, pp. 207–216.

30 Johanna Drucker, *Iliazd: A Meta-Biography of a Modernist*, p. 66. In another article Drucker argued that Iliazd's artistic energy found its final gesture through expression "in the book, making full use of its capacity to function as an art form." Johanna Drucker, 'Iliazd and the Book as an Art Form',

The Journal of Decorative and Propaganda Arts, Vol. 7, Winter, 1988, p. 36.

31 On the relationship of Lenin with Dimitri Snegaroff and Volf Chalit, two typographers who established l'Imprimerie Union, see the excellent website dedicated to the history of the printing house: https://imprimerie-union.org/annees-russes/lenine.

Introduction

I LIA ZDA

at the Birthday Party

Are you familiar with the artist Yakovlev?[1] The one
that invariably walks around with his cane, clutching
the dog's head silver knob to his heart. This is the
way he was pictured in a photograph by Shumov,
also a famous figure on St. Jacques Street.[2] So that
same Yakovlev carries on a friendly narrative on the
unusual, on how, having awoken in the morning, he
discovered, being laid not only in his shoes, not only
his smoking jacket, but also his overcoat. Whether
he had a hat on his head (a very bad sign and omen,
in the opinion of artist Larionov, who of course
would have been giddy with delight if he found out
that Yakovlev had a hat on lying in his bed) – now,
Yakovlev was silent on the matter of the hat. You
sense the electricity in the atmosphere. The artist is
asked – how did this happen to you? The response is
amaranthine – nothing surprising, I was at a birthday
party the other night.

Here you have an episode and a dissociation, so
eloquent. Is Paris at fault for Yakovlev speaking this
language, when a child's pleasure does not matter – a
birthday turns into a bottom of birth [дно рождения],
whereafter a man goes to sleep without removing a
single article of clothing, since every shot has already
been taken. On the other hand, silence on the subject
of the hat, to deny Larionov the opportunity of hope.
And all this because the conversation is being heard
by me, the hero of the Iliazda.

What is the matter? What sort of new Achilles
has appeared, and what sort of litmus test am I to
make people speak their mind so frankly, uncovering

their contradictions and discords? The role of the provocateur is revealed immediately. One that will inevitably pit everyone against each other, hated by everyone, one that sees nastiness everywhere. I ask of Talov, "tell me, does Ginger not suffer from constipation? Does his poetry talk about it too much?" Talov – "yes, he does."[3] Question – "and Parnakh seems to be able to have pleasure from a mere sight." Talov – "yes, yes, there are stories of him walking down the Champs-Elysées, laying eyes on someone – A Cloud in Trousers." Isn't it disgusting to delve into everything. And isn't it disgusting to bring intimate conversations with artists and poets out to the public and speak of devil-knows-what. Every time. The blockhead keeps spreading bad airs everywhere, and nobody is the wiser where all this vitriol comes from. The canary sings too sweetly, and apes virtue willy-nilly. But such a scumbag in reality.

Here is what I shall say to you: we are equally distant from attempts at building a new art and from attempts at destroying it, and from any creative recipes whatsoever. "Art must" – the imperative didactic, with which old and new schools have been obsessed in past years – no longer exists. Art does not owe anything to anybody, and not for the sole reason that it is aimless etc. Art for the sake of art – a formula for the aesthetes – is a recipe just like the Futurists' wishes in response to questions of the spirit. The same didactic, with the appearance of involuntariness, is the same as a worker seeking employment from life – nobody is forcing one. In all

cases, the same line of action is foretold. I declare
that such a line does not exist, and can no longer
exist. Art is not aimless, it may be, or better, turn out
to be practical, or it may not, as the case may be. The
answer to questions of the spirit – perhaps, perhaps
not, a new sensation, the contemporary human –
the rest is excellent; some old archaism is not bad
either. What matters is not the yardstick, plurality
is what matters. Art does not fit in any framework,
not even the framework of art. Not through lack
of integrity, as someone said to me today. This is
something I dubbed *everythingism* [*toutité*] back in
the year 1913. The same as squaring the circle – an
unsolvable question. Explained, if you like, by the fact
that the operational planes of recipes, fundamentals,
definitions are different from the nature of art,
which is relatively irrational and therefore escapes
definition. It may be the other way round. The past
few years have been devoted enough to the matter of
originality and imitation. The notion of the copy was
thus demolished. What is being copied, the object,
is always an object of art, be it a painting or a line
of motion. So we have parted ways with the hefty
jurisprudence left to us by the nineteenth century.

But we do have a different criterion that we have
been unable to do away with so far. Meanwhile, any talk
of whether art is junk or a soulful thing, what we should
destroy and what we should build up, and all rhetoric
around which we shall continue revolve for hundreds
of moons to come, fails to meet the goal, until one tiny
but touchy matter is raised – one of talent and gift.

  Iliazda at the Birthday Party

Whether inspiration is necessary for art or not, is something to which we still have different answers. But here is the question of the gift. What shall we do with it? Sudeykin, after leaving my lecture about the House on Shit, says to Lipchitz: "that is all true, but he is talented."[4] Lipchitz responds: "sure, nobody questions that." I apologise to the authors of the conversation if I have conveyed it with insufficient precision. But, as a favour to me, let everything remain in place.

Here are the opinions that require some investigation. Does a gift matter to art? You may say, yes. Is a gift enough, Lipchitz says, no. Sudeykin is essentially in agreement with Lipchitz, but in the game the three of us play with that stupid art, makes his remise at me: "Zdanevich is talented, he will prove himself still." Lipchitz, of course, leaves the question open: "no need to peer into the future, the turn is mine. Allow me. I play the ace of diamonds."

Let us reveal our cards. Five minutes of attention and patience. I shall try to explain my complete self. Mr Gurgenov issued a book of poetry in Moscow with his own portrait, titled *Gurgenov's Poetry*.[5] Despite all his desire to write, he hardly succeeds. There can be no talk of Gurgenov's gift. He barely tortured out several pages, and that was his life's only feat. Here is what he writes, by the way:

"A maiden once sat at a creek
The word husbands she did think
And suddenly went pale

          Iliazda at the Birthday Party

And notices a horse before her
That puts her on its back
A beauty full of passion's fervour
And trots over mountains
And trots over valleys
Carrying the exquisite beauty far away."

The sense of permission and relief with which the poet finishes, having rushed to the end of his poem, are as expressive as a horse's gallop. I cannot deny this poem the luxury of overlooking it. Another poet, Melnikov, issued a book in Berlin which he called *Demon: Eastern Novella.*[6] In the preface, the author declares that the source for his poem was Lermontov's opera *Demon*, and that his youthful childish soul would grace the public with multiple revelations of this kind. Lermontov's *Demon* is interpreted thus. For instance, Lermontov writes:

"A saddened demon, exile's spirit,
Once flew above a sinful land."

As Melnikov puts it:

"A random demon, exile's spirit,
Once flew above a splendid land etc."

Sometimes the lines stretch out. By substituting some words with others in this manner, the author takes the path of contrast. And while the *Demon* of Lermontov makes no impression but bland today,

    Iliazda at the Birthday Party

Melnikov's demon conceals no small amount of sharp propositions:

> "And the monotonous splish-splashing
> Of gushing streams in deep ravines."

Terentiev expended quite a lot of effort on substantiating that creative technique – his own, Kruchenykh's, Pushkin's and Marinetti's, which the latter would call *imagination sans fils* [imagination without strings] and Terentiev dubbed the *l'itinéraire global* [global itinerary, or route of sphericity, which according to Kruchenykh: "The steamboat excited by the route of sphericity"].

"Stuffed oak" or "twirling imitation fetters" – all wonderful chance events.[7] Balmont was also amazed by the Spanish women with their "I am all ice and fire."[8] That black flame sun of Tyutchev and again Lermontov in his *Demon* was all the ice and fire, neither day nor night nor dark nor light. But this game of contrast, foreshadowing the route of sphericity, is nothing compared to the richness of form Melnikov produced in his *Demon.* This necessitates the acknowledgement of his book as one of the most notable works of recent years. I regret not having this book with me in Paris to provide more quotations.

∗∗∗

Picabia has a Japanese engraving hung in his living room with cracked glass.[9] Pointing at the pattern of

     Iliazda at the Birthday Party

cracks, brother Francis marvels. Does he know where such marvel leads? In 1913, in St. Petersburg, the late Vladimir Markov issued a little book called *Faktura* [Texture]. He writes not about texture, but about structure, and has no grasp of the things he is talking about. But that does not matter. What piques one's curiosity are the pages on which he talks about the role of chance in the creation of artistic work, about how good it is to plaster newsprint over a canvas, rip off the paper, and make use of the arrangement of random spots that results. He says the same of Japanese vases. Children's magazines often include images made with splotches – several random blots producing a drawing with proper handling. Did the *pompiers* who invited the donkey to paint the *Sunset over the Adriatic* know that they were, by chance, committing the same apology of chance as would Markov and Picabia.[10] The name *Oslinyi Khvost* [Donkey's Tail] was adopted by Larionov's group.[11] But they had a different approach to the matter. And finally, Terentiev culminated with one of his nonsensical tools [*erundovykh orudii*]: collecting the errors of typesetters, distorting critics, who are at times geniously foolish etc.[12]

Of course, the apology of chance is not the apology of chance at the expense of structure and composition. The construction of things is not affected by this. This is a specimen article. It is only one manifestation of the conviction I am promoting, that not only recipes play no role in creativity and art. [Remember Melnikov, Gurgenov and the cracked

 Iliazda at the Birthday Party

glass.] In art, no role is also played by something different – the gift of the master. It is of no consequence whatsoever whether he is talented or mediocre.

What is "geniously foolish"? If chance does play a role, and results are known from results, then the fact of the master's ability to handle his material, whether he is gifted with creative potential to a sufficient degree, has no say in the matter. This is not about names, about the pillars of art. The quoted poem by Gurgenov outweighs Balmont's profuse writings, although the gift of the latter is beyond doubt. I would even say that the gift is most often related to mediocre things, to eclecticism, while form changes and evolves within things that are insignificant in terms of their preliminary tension and have unparalleled heft in terms of their ultimate effect. They wanted to break free from everything, they shouted about all sorts of destruction, and construction, but they could not solve the question of talent in art. Several days ago, I had an interview with the artist Viktor Bart.[13] In conversation, he would repeat the word "talent" most often. The word was heard in reference to Tintoretto and El Greco and Cézanne. And, finally, Bart himself. Then Bart said: "I have not resolved one question: do you, Zdanevich, have a talent or not. I am looking closely, it is not clear, we shall see." The same things were spoken by Salomea Andronikova in Tbilisi, as it is written in "41°" – a fashionable topic in salon talks remains the question of whether Ilya Zdanevich is a poet or not.

     Iliazda at the Birthday Party

The authoritative arbiter – Salomea Andronikova
– rules in the negative.[14] This is the same as the
conversation with Romov near the métro Vavin – the
centre of the world. Romov, a delicate little gent,
avoided answering the question – Zdanevich is smart,
the question of talent was not raised, after all.[15]

I would like to end the suffering of Bart, calm
Romov, thank Sudeykin for the valiant defence, spare
Lipchitz the discussions, and agree with Andronikova
– leave it, gentlemen, I am giftless, I am not talented,
I am perfectly aware of it, and everyone around me is
aware of it. Let us cease the game of blind and buff
and be frank. We must renounce the harmful manner
of contemplation – what if something here is quite
for a reason. There is nothing. I am well-read, smart,
educated, but utterly talentless in poetry, torturing
out small bits, with much effort, poorly, hiding behind
the cloak of zaum, let us put this matter to rest. But
this is exactly why I am aspiring to your attention.

Were I a poet with some talent, everything would
be so natural and simple. Marked by fate, born this
way, all aces in hand. But I am playing a game with
you which know not how. And that is the deal. As
someone without a gift, I have my place in poetry
(as discovered by Romov, whose magazine also has
its place), and this place is sprawling and expanding.
Near the Symbolists, how are themselves becoming
(of) symbol(s) and contemporary pompes and
sucklings of Modernism, my position is through no
fault of mine deemed threatening and utterly nobody
knows how this muddle will end. A matter of chance,

     Iliazda at the Birthday Party

what patterns may come out. I myself have nothing, I
am naked as a jaybird, both materially and spiritually.
If circumstances favour, the bungling boor, as I was
reasonably called a decade ago, will swim, if not – will
sink. So far, the circumstances do favour, and I am in
luck. Here is something for you to ponder, whereafter
we can resume our disrupted discussions about art.

I remain faithful to what I said at the beginning.
Boundaries are impossible. There were times – like
those of Veronese – when talent was required.
Now, vulgarity is not too wrong in saying nothing is
necessary for one to be a contemporary master:
the centre has shifted. Now, truly, you can possess
nothing. Which is why I was born into this world
in 1894.[16] Last Sunday I was at the delightful
Shukhaevs', celebrating 28 years since my birth.[17] I
was also at my birthday party.

Fate brings us again to the birthday. This
forces me to add this: not only is talent of no need
to contemporary art, but, in stronger terms – it is
excluded from it. They say the visual arts have come
to a contradiction in their key tasks. And what is a gift
if not, first and foremost, the capacity to solve these
tasks? Once again – the criterion is not absolute, the
question is about the conditions of the day. In the
days of Veronese, talent may have been more than
useful, sincerely necessary. Because the path of
development in art was such that accomplishing his
feats was only possible with a gift. Now, things are
different. The proposition that the arts have come to
a fundamental contradiction includes two aspects.

   Iliazda at the Birthday Party

Firstly: art in this state of affairs is impossible to a gift that cannot suffer this contradiction. I tend least of all towards paradoxical propositions. I assert deductively that talent, to a contemporary master, is harmful because it cannot give anything positive, yet brings heaps of harm. If literature written on fences, the strains of mediocrities contain more living water than the creations of talents, this is because art is currently undergoing a phase of this sort. Flowing from this are conciseness, difficulty and constipations. And I assert that, due to its structure of chance mounting of form, dilettantism, tortuousness and theorising, contemporary art is the art of the talentless. And I am entirely in my place.

Here you have the result. Lermontov gushed creativity – he stuffed his *Demon* chock full of flaws of some sort. Now, a customs office pencil-pusher has come and rewritten his *Demon,* which turns out more lively and valuable to us.[18] Such is contemporary art. Now you understand why I am aspiring to your attention. I do not want to play hide-and-seek, to pretend and allow irrelevant matters to be discussed. And I should like to say to my critics: you, gentlemen, are talented beyond question, but I am no worse than yourselves. And as much as Fatma Hanum might object to such an equation, I insist on it.[19]

The first point of interest on our departure from the bottom of birth [дно рождения] is the fact that I was born with three teeth. My frightened parents knew not what to endeavour at the sight of a newborn gnashing its teeth and biting at such a

 Iliazda at the Birthday Party

young age. That was the first impression I made upon seeing the light of day.

I do not know why Terentiev decided my childhood years are of nobody's concern. He is right, I was exceptionally handsome, and that alone makes the story interesting. Then again, Tereshkovich[20] still finds me good-looking, while Ginger, whom I met many, many years ago, has now recognised me by my attractive belly. But we drive onwards.

I was dressed as a girl.[21] My mother would not accept the fact that she bore a son instead of a daughter. Her diary says: "gave birth to a girl – Ilya, hair – black, colour – dark blue." So I wore my curly hair down to my shoulders. Every night, my nanny Zina would craft a pile of curlpapers by taking out book after book from a shelf in grandfather's library, and I would spend the night with several pounds of paper on my head. Thus, the shelves were cleared of Pushkin, Griboedov, Derzhavin, Gogol, one after another. In my dreams, their writings would enter my head, and I gradually turned into a poet.

"Too curlies" said the inspector for the Y-sk gymnasium [preparatory school] when in 1902 I was taken there to brave the relevant exam. But I was so charming that the examination was allowed, and my appearance became the first ever case of co-education in Russia. It is now commonplace, but my trip to the gymnasium wearing a skirt had caused a sensation. Attempts to make a girl out of me were incessant. But I made use of my privilege, often entering the girls' gymnasium, attending locations

Iliazda at the Birthday Party

spelling out "ladies only", causing massive admiration there as well. My friendship with my girlfriends lasted until I caused harm to one of them. I was already twelve at the time. My situation had become unbearable. I was beaten twice, and the ladies made a statement to the police. By a ruling of a justice of the peace, my parents were to dress me in trousers.

What is left of that period in life when I was a girl? Several photographic cards and the soft sign [ь] I put at the end of my surname on festive occasions. The response was catastrophic. I went to have my curls trimmed. The story turned out the opposite of Samson's. My hatred for the past had grown to such an extent that I decided to stop walking forwards, something I used to do as a girl, and began walking backwards, like devils knows what. The Dadaists have a saying, however: when I stand with my back to you, you are being studied by my arse. But my arse was sightless. At a seaside swim, my manner of running with my back led to a fall off a cliff. I did not die.

Since then, everything in me has petered out. My feet and legs have shifted, I stopped growing. My morals have deteriorated just like my body. From a charming creature with a touch of genius I turned into something dull, talentless, bilious and vicious. I became insufferable in school. My attitude to lessons also changed – from among the best students, I became the worst. It all was accompanied by prophetic chattiness. My poetic upbringing of curlpapers had evaporated, the memory had faded. I became the despicable degenerate I remain. That

    Iliazda at the Birthday Party

is what no longer being a girl means. I moved to St. Petersburg then, where I opened the *School of Kisses*.

Igor Terentiev, my kind and glorious biographer, has included me in the community of saints. I do not know if it is the case. We will talk about it later. Here is what he writes about me:

> "Ilya Zdanevich came of age somewhere
> between the Caucasus, St. Petersburg, Moscow
> and Paris, where he would make appearances
> with public lectures, recitations of other people's
> poetry, and just so. Mutual acquaintances share
> anecdotes about the 'School of Kisses' allegedly
> established by Ilya somewhere up North,
> talk about his brilliant speech in Kislovodsk,
> carousing, lechery, impudence and the jovial
> nature of this kind-hearted, egotistic, wry,
> sentimental, reserved, hot-headed and criminal
> young man. Inspiring in people not only respect,
> contempt, anger, but also participance, Ilya
> would hear much useful advice from relatives
> and friends, who always felt that the youth were
> destined for great heights."[22]

How fair are these peaceful and calm narratives by Saint Terentiev from my second reality? The School of Kisses was the first league of love in Russia. It culminated in two homicides, three suicides and four orations. I shall name the orators – each of them took a path for the worse. They were Khlebnikov, Mayakovsky, Kruchenykh, and – Lady Mary forgive

me – Ehrenburg, christened Ilya in my honour. I shut
the School as one shuts a mouth, and loathed the
land. The sole of the boot did not seem sufficient
to me. That was the *baignoire* of the theatre of life. I
added three centimetres to my sole and climbed to
the *bel-étage*. Then I made a shoe-shiner on Nevsky
Prospekt out of myself. You may have heard about
the silly philosophy I developed back then around
the boot.[23] In Moscow, they slashed my wrists over
the boot and Venus. Thus came the era historians
call the era of the boot in Russia. Everything ended
with the famous story of the trousers. We turn up our
trousers in contempt as well. But better to cut them
off. So I took scissors and cut them off. The trousers
wore down quickly. I cut them again. I had to slacken
my suspenders. Day by day cutting off the bottoms
of my trousers down to nothing like this, I soon
discovered that contempt leads to an insufficiency
of suspenders, and trousers must be worn not at the
waist but at the rump (one of the ladies currently in
attendance once admitted that the best part of a
horse's body was the rump, as is a donkeys').

And thusly, after some time had passed, the
bottoms of my trousers had to be worn so low down
that I would not take off my coat and barely moved –
the first to make a fashion statement of *entraves*.[24]
Soon I was unable to walk, and the cut-down trousers
were good for nothing. They once dropped on Nevsky
Prospekt; I was arrested, and they spent a lot of time
wondering how someone could walk in athletic shorts
of such diminutive length. After this silly story, which

    Iliazda at the Birthday Party

played the most decisive role in the latter half of my life, all was lost for me.

I killed, killed again, killed more, then killed once again and went to prison. After leaving, I was in an old crone's keep. I robbed her (Raskolnikov has been copied from my likeness), but was only caught in a pocket theft. I hit rock bottom. I only survived through refusing drink and chastity. However, I was fired from a typesetting shop after a scandal. Accused of embezzlement. Lawlessness confused with hairlessness. I painted my face, purporting to be a poet from 1912 till 1917, never having been one. Then again, I continue to purport to be a poet without being one. But there, in St. Petersburg, all was lost. I was accused of literary fraud, and Balmont loathed me. *Sovremennye Zapiski* (Contemporary Papers) – you know, the Socialist Revolutionary papers currently in print – accepted me as a floor polisher. I rewrote Kerensky's articles for him.[25] Zenzinov thought the world of me.[26] But it was still a time of autocracy, and they were powerless. I was imprisoned, and the second streak of my life was finished.

The revolution knocked down the doors of prisons, and I came out. Thus began the third epoch of my lifetime.

Fraud was no longer profitable. You be the judge. Alexandre Benois wanted to establish a Ministry of Art. I conducted an energetic agitation campaign in 1917, organising the Union of Artists. I was active, agitating, and gave the famous speech on 23 March

Iliazda at the Birthday Party

at the Mikhailovsky Theatre, while Benois failed.[27]
But when they started electing the Union Council,
there was no seat. An art critic – are you joking?
Having written only a single critical book in all his life,
and even that on Larionov and Goncharova, and even
that under a pen name.[28] A poet? Nobody ever heard
his poetry – he has none to show for it. When all the
art activists left the enormous session chamber to
their election rooms, I, facilitator and decorator, was
left alone. I had nowhere to go. I sat down at a desk.
And I cried. Cried for the first time in my life.

As a girl, I used to suffer menstruations, there
was blood but with no murder. I have now committed
myself to a bloodless murder of everything – all
of life, literature, the Sologubovs, the Russian
language.[29] Fraud was no longer an option. I wrote
and staged *Yanko, King of Albania*. In his book,
Terentiev remarks on the fact as follows:

> "The young man listened to everyone and
> heeded every bit of their advice, allotting a week,
> a month, or a year to each. At the same time,
> with nobody's appreciation — of his own kind
> nature alone — Ilya became a poet."[30]

Of my own kind nature – what else can I say. That
would be like me reading these lectures of my own
kind nature. If I could be doing nothing and living on
credit (you and I live on credit, Bart says to me), I
would be doing nothing, just like the half-year before.
But fraud is no longer a possibility. I have the soul of

a fraudster. But I am too cowardly for impudence. My motto is – be fraudulent without impudence.

These are the lifestyle circumstances in which my art should have taken shape. I am an utter lowlife. I have no prejudice or morals not by virtue of overcoming them through ascension to some planes, they simply melted away. In the aspect of revolution, I take a place (once again, the right place) that cannot be defined precisely. I am being condemned in every camp. Sharshun said my mezzo-soprano sounds lonely.[31] I am an ethical and literary misfit that irritates everyone with his misfittery. That is my type. And here is how it is expressed.

Kruchenykh, in his analysis of contemporary poetry, wrote the story of three Byllockians (мамудийцев).[32] Last time, I mentioned that Saltykov-Shchedrin has this: "Take a poster and go to Byllockia."[33] From this follows the country of Byllockia [Mamudia], which in Persian means a small gold coin. You know what it means for a contemporary poet to flee from the woman. Raymond Duncan-Marinetti earlier praught *mepris (de) la femme*.[34] This *contempt* led to the development of criminal stories. All the charms of poetry after a bath have appeared.[35] Three poets arrived for the final combat. The first was Khlebnikov, the second Mayakovsky. We have seen Khlebnikov's portrait. And we know Mayakovsky's as his Lilya Brik. I came third.

Kruchenykh dispassionately dissects the essence of the third Byllockian. The theme of the "bl" [blya], dissociated within and transformed from the

Iliazda at the Birthday Party

flowing to the explosive "br", indicates his place. The Decembrists – remember December for Tyutchev – give us Mayakovsky's dreary decembry evening. The hulk shouts in his bass: "only two words thrive and thicken: 'bastard' and something else, perhaps 'borsch'."[36] He boasted – a thief and a cardshark, then begged: "I did not steal any silver spoons!" He claimed he would have Napoleon on a leash, that "I could have my way with anyone, then spit right in her eye."[37] Look what came of it.

A page is missing here – thrown out by a *femme de ménage* at my Rue Zacharie hotel, No. 20 – so I must disrupt the narrative. The lost page said, I think: Khlebnikov would threaten to drown you in the saliva of love. And how did he finish? Resting near Mashuk and Ehrenburg promising him the fate of today's Vyacheslav Ivanov.[38]

I beg for mercy. While I spent a week looking for the lost page at my residence, unable to continue the lecture, which remains destined to no end, Blaise Cendrars,[39] who was with me in Brancusi at the Café du Parnasse,[40] showed me the *Vešč'* – Ehrenburg's magazine.[41] And we are unable to finish with the story of the three Byllockians before we discuss him.

The life of Ehrenburg and his activities are defined by two facts – that, being a follower of Symbolism and not knowing where to latch on to, he met Francis Jammes;[42] and – his meeting with me in a period of his life that will be addressed shortly. We do not know Ehrenburg from Jammes before the verses about the eves.[43] He brought these verses to the city of Tbilisi, where at the time I had been elected president of the 41° Republic. Some of those in attendance recall this brilliant epoch in my life. Thus, Ehrenburg paid visits to 41°, came here, from there to here, away from there etc.[44]

Gentlemen, contemporary art drives mediocrities, not talents. Ehrenburg is talented, which is why he is so out of place. When he writes under a steamboat that it is a heap of hay, he testifies to a wonderful soul flowering within him in search of amazement. When, under the pseudonym of Jean *Salo* (I shall not analyse the French spelling of this surname, the wit of it is dull), he calls 41° a Dadaist pox, he is mistaken, because pox never causes such an elevation in temperature.[45] When he presents a rhymed declaration of Mayakovskiness and drags Pasternak out by his ears – to prove that everyone in Russia is Scythian – God, how talented it all is. I understand that my lack of talent spoils the magnificent picture of Russian grandeur. The priests all so gifted, a house on shit, pleasant, but then there are people who spoil the entire thing. No matter, there is a way out. I am not Russian. I have a Georgian passport, and I am a Georgian.[46]

The picture of Doomsday will hang on this wall. On it, Ehrenburg will ascend to heaven with pockets full of the trinkets stolen from the naïve Frenchmen so forcefully instituting a spiritual reaction.

But the lost page has been redeemed, and you are left to sue the concierge for me, instead of talking business, feeding you such unbelievably talented muck as Ehrenburg.

Iliazda at the Birthday Party

My position is not the position of Mayakovsky nor the position of Khlebnikov. It is the ancient December of the Decembrists, it is "bri"[47] (Dostoyevsky's "bri bri" and "mabish" and "æpuzy"[48]) I have combined with "yu" (Ю)[49], with moisture, the pronoun of love. Bryusov had nothing from this "bryu" except his name, and the story with *bryuki* [trousers] had happened to me recently. Instead of battling Lilith, the woman, I took the path of least resistance – as a criminal and lover of easy money. Instead of Mayakovsky's dry, erect perpendicular – dreary decembry evening – I gave them bryu – cartilage. You cannot do anything with a soft piece of cartilage, everybody knows that. Thus was declared the proposition that poetry is an assassination attempt by unsuitable [unprofitable] means.[50] Everything is pulled off to the end. A thought does not live in a brain such as mine. I am bare as a bone, I have nothing to hide, I have no need for either Mayakovsky's bravado or Khlebnikov's mystery. My vices are obvious. I do not wish to conquer anything because I know I shall conquer nothing anyway.

Y [Ы] – a letter that does not begin words, says the uncouth abecedary.[51] I have created the entire 'yts language' – what an abomination – 'yts language' [ывонный язык], and wrote *Yanko, King of Albania* in it. As someone of no talent and lazy, writing it took me a long time and two sittings. I started writing it in prison during the old regime. I sent the first version to the censors for printing. Censor Rimsky-Korsakov, son of the composer, I think he is here

in Paris, picked nits with the phrase "yu ass… [ю
асёл…]" and, believing this to be a parody of a royal
personage, barred *Yanko* from print. The Revolution
gave me freedom. I got to work writing the second
version, spending my days in Tavricheskoe and at the
Kseshinskaya Mansion.[52] "Haram bazham glam" was
written after Kerensky's speech upon accepting the
portfolio of the Minister for Justice against the wishes
of the soviets[53] – and "ae bie bao biu bao" followed
Lenin's speech about who profits from the war.[54] My
vileness, cynicism and lack of principle forced me to
flee St. Petersburg. In April 1917, I left the city for the
Caucasus,[55] where I was being awaited by long-time
friend di Lado, a Parisian painter – whose drawings
at the gallery Licorne on rue La Boétie', soon to open,
you must not forget to attend.[56]

    Gentlemen, in the depths of the ocean there
are also fish living under the enormous pressure of
the water. Their forms are grotesque, and, removed
from their strata up or out, they break and die. The
environment of zaum poetry is the environment
of enormous pressure of sound, and the creatures
dwelling in these conditions cannot be distinguished
by forms reasonable for the mundane strata. Which
is why, in the environment of 'yts language', only
freaks, cretins can thrive, and the author makes no
attempt to even speak ironically of his characters.
I want you to understand why, scorned by God and
people, I create personae in my own image, unwilling
and incapable of stepping outside the circle of these
vices, diseases, these criminals, thieves, idiots and

    Iliazda at the Birthday Party

nitwits. I am a person devoid of all creativity. Once I had ascertained that playing a poet without doing anything was not possible, I did what was easiest for me to do – wrote down some gibberish and imparted my qualities to the characters. Of course no society can tolerate me.

If *Yanko* could not be printed in St. Petersburg, I issued it in Tbilisi, in May 1918. That is how I got my own book. There you have the secret of my exploits and my youth. Does not matter that I was already famous when Mayakovsky timidly started performing back in 1913.[57] I was able to stall the start of my literary activity for five years. And next year I shall only be celebrating five years of literary activity, whereas some, who began along with me, will already be celebrating ten years of inactivity. Here is what Terentiev wrote about *Yanko*:

> "The plot is simple enough: a vagabond yanko encounters some bandits in the middle of a quarrel. As someone entirely alien and impersonal — yanko is coerced into kinghood. He is fearful. He is glued to the throne with synditicone, tries to unstick, is helped by some austrian named yrental: they both shout "wota", but there is no water, and yanko dies by the knife of the bandits, letting out a 'foof'. That is all. A story worthy of a nativity or a puppet show."
> "Here we can observe Russia in the 19th century."

        Iliazda at the Birthday Party

"Gutchino, oak cupboard and Serafim Sarovski."
"Ilya Zdanevich's voice is heard in 'yanko' well
enough, using the letter 'y' as the root to easily
reach the upper-register 'y':
"albejnjen lengweg livs alongsaid rushn stems
from yt."
"yts language uncovers all intrinsically russian
capabilities, which however have not been used
in "yanko": there is not a single woman in it, not a
single "yi" — not a drop of moisture."[58]

He is slightly mistaken – there is a woman, but
she is a flea. The third final battle with Lilya is only
beginning. The flea was not noticed and I was
suspected. Time to take a rest. With my dear friend
di Lado we left for Turkey, where we would wander
around villages, studying ancient paintings and
architecture. One day, while we lived in Ishkhan,
soldiers going towards the front brought us a single
issue of a newspaper – we had not seen one for over
two months. In it, I read an article by my brother, the
artist, about the military death of artist Ledentu.[59]
    If you are unfamiliar with the name of this
painter, that does not mean anything, you will know
it soon enough. This entire stream of artistic ideas
I am expounding comes from him. He was the most
powerful figure among Russian painters. I sat at a
table in Ishkhan and cried. For the second and last
time in my life.
    It was clear. The war was coming to an end. The
circle of ideas that began in Albania – Prince Wied –

so-called "принц Вид Дурацкий" [Prince Wied of Durres, or Prince Looking Foolish] – had been played out.[60] The war had been spent. The revolution came into its current cycle.

But authors are sluggish and dull, especially when they are talentless like myself, in reflecting the ideas that come to pass. Di Lado and I returned to Tbilisi. I opened the 41° University with Kruchenykh, who had come there. I am now continuing this cause in Paris. I had become sick of *Yanko*. I needed to look for new excuses. The woman had grown into a bride, according to Eastern laws and customs, 14 years were quite enough.

I had to write again. Inspiration did not come. There was no love and nowhere for it to come from. I happily managed to contract typhoid fever. Now that is when the temperature increases to 41°. Sensing bouts of anal creativity, I addressed my disease at a lecture and excused myself from the oratorium.

Typhoid was indubitable. Doctors prescribed enemas and a compress. At the time I wrote the drama *Donkey for Rent* – the famous compress of woman. Yanko's dryness gave way to unprecedented softness and moisture. Two grooms in eager competition expressing their feelings for a bride, a donkey doing the same. She expresses hers to one, the other, the donkey, the ass. Anal eroticism reaches its peak and finishes. "Zokhna could have taken the ass for the human and vice versa by means unknown."[61] Everything was put on the line, and I won. "A tenderness record has been set by Ilya Zdanevich, brimming with delight."[62]

     Iliazda at the Birthday Party

Khlebnikov would take time manufacturing
saliva, while out of nowhere came "yupyapik", which
outgushed from him with no difficulty. "All obscenely
love-filled words eel, ooze, woo, ess in wanton
jubilation…"[63]:

> "napYAlyaya, kIYUs' yaslyuslYAyka vbil'E piizYAti
> ibUn'kubun' kEyu khalYAvay pEk
> iffYAfsy tsviYUtyu unAbi lYUp'
> gyaenYAy talEstis mavzEpit kazYUku kachYUch
> razivAyu yupAyak fEyki padvYAski…"[64]

Donkey for Rent was followed by the resurrection of
a woman. Everyone comes back to their first love.
Which is why I hit upon to *Eastr Ailand* [Ostraf Pashi].
What I had as a girl is not menstruation.
    And why is this period not eradicated in my
pieces? Lilith the Woman – broad of a certain
age. This was the third drama in the aslaabliche
[*dunkeeness,* donkey aspect, *or asspect*]:

> "The third drama of the "aslaabliche"
> [dunkeeness] cycle [*Eastr Ailand*, 1919] features
> a more committed transformation of human
> into donkey: the host speaks of the 'eastr ailand'
> characters with near affection: 'Merchant a
> veritable ass crætor more so two and a half
> stone broads also tripe.'
> Quite the joyful drama: everybody dies and
> everybody resurrects — period… one mons!!
> Two and a ½ broads (character reference)

     Iliazda at the Birthday Party

– first – earth-dusted mother; old crone's makeup. Second – sister in law with hysteria in a bathroom.
The half – a complete œ!
And the crætor's kindest words are dedicated to the half:
'meadowy
laidown spanker
doey'."[65]

Now you understand how I resolved the difficulties had by the Byllockians [Mamudi] Mayakovsky and Khlebnikov. Lilith, Lilya – is me – Ilya, Lyu as they call and called me. In life I had been a girl, later a boy. This gave me the opportunity to fight my own self, biting my tail, to battle as a man the woman in me and as a woman the man in me. But is that the purpose of the transformation, and was I not apparently Zdanevich at the start of my life, a woman apparently, apparently zga, zga apparently [*Zga Yakaby*, 1920]. Does the resurrection of woman not solve this problem with the novel hermaphrodite of talentless and deceitful, unscrupulous and impermanent Zdanevich.

And I wrote the fourth "dunkeeness" (аслаабличий) drama. It was clear. The woman is the donekey and the other way round. Where else would this muck go? But woman after broad is already a crone.

In my first lecture on the House on Shit, I already read to you *Zga Yakaby*. Romov said that these Massenets.[66] Allow me another few extractions.

A crone sits at a mirror. In it you see a girl. That is I.
The girl becomes a young man. That is I also. The
crone becomes a man. Also myself. Here is how the
saga, so benevolent at first, ends:

> "ayOuyou zgAgaga flApped
> tralalAed HoUst
> bIInd mAn ritErns finO."[67]

But all imaginations die, and all visions do too.
Kruchenykh discovered that the final verses of *Zga* are
constructed like *Woe from Wit*": "haAssous exilsus
baaYU ichewÆs baYU aYUyu zgAgaga flYApped
dollielEllies [hashAkai vYisus' baaYU yazhuyiYAyahi
baYU aYUyu zgAgaga syuchYAli lyalilEli хашАкай
вЫисусь бааЮ яжуйиЯяхи баЮ аЮю згАгага
сючЯли лялилЕли"].[68] This I had stolen from
Griboedov: "The day is gone, and with it / the smoke,
the fumes, the spirits, / that used to drown my soul."
After the latest dirty trick with Lilith, from whom I stole
the name Ilya, she had nothing left to do but die. It
was I, Iliazd, that died for a second time, in the second
period of my life. All that remains now is to return to
the problem of Le Dentu that occupied me since time
immemorial. And, on my deathbed, once the woman
within me had died entirely, wrote the final drama from
the "dunkeeness" sequence – *Ledentu as Beacon*
[*lidantYU fAram*]. Give dying Zdanevich his burial
rites. After *Eastr Ailand* comes a second resurrection.
And what profligacy leads me to sacrilege instead
of communion right before my death. Instead of the

        Iliazda at the Birthday Party

Holy Spirit's descent to the apostles, which caused
their glossolalia, a holy fart [запредухий, or hind wind]
descended upon me. And the second coming does not
give me what it gives you:

> "in the name of the lord donkey
> and the holy hind wind
> and the uterine frenzy,
> the monotremes stage
> the second coming
> as the end of all ends."[69]

If a woman is a man, why not become monotremes
ourselves. The last rites are given to me, the man
deceased, and him, the man deceased, and her, the
woman deceased.

> "dEEr sltizens
> wAr prophesYd bY Olga lyashkOva's klddren klkd
> thE bAket   jAst sOU"[70]

I shall not read from my yet unpublished, unread
drama today, about me being Orpheus, ripped to
shreds by lubbers, descending into hell. Commercial
interests and your tiredness call for a separate night
devoted to that.

Gentlemen, canonical portraits depict me, a
goner and a saint, with wings. Terentiev wrote about
me: "an angel of compact stature and an insolent
singer."[71] Sudeykin says: "angel milliork".[72] In the
portrait I shall of course ask to be drawn by none

other than Fotinsky, I shall have wings as well.[73] Goncharova also drew my portrait.[74] This is because, gentlemen, let me reiterate, I am long dead. I used to be a rascal, but my chrysalis has incubated an angel.

A knock on the door just came – that's the *femme de ménage* – she found the lost page. Here it is – I select things that were not written in it:

My poetry is the dénouement of all those tendencies sheltered in my precursors. I perceive poetry as the pearl disease of a disease. A dead body continues to grow hair in the grave, and when shaven corpses were disturbed some days or weeks later, they were found to be bearded. Art is long dead. My giftless creativity – with all its strains for the sake of gathering several curious onlookers in this hall – is a beard growing on the face of a dead body. Dadaists are feasting worms: that is our cardinal difference. They came from outside; I sprout from a body that was never alive. Should the casket be opened, they will see the beard, but the chance is slim. I create because I am branded with the seal of generations, because degenerations of the species ultimately produced an unprincipled, scummy, criminal misfit such as myself, that is able to live solely of spiritual fraud, one that corrupts mentally and physically. Do not let me disturb you after death. Do not allow my organisation to pollute your happiness, talents, and air.

Iliazda at the Birthday Party

1 Alexander Evgenievich Yakovlev (1887–1938) was a Russian neo-classicist painter and a member of The World of Art [Мир искусства] . From 1920 until his death he lived in Paris.

2 Pyotr Ivanovich Shumov (1872–1936) lived in Paris from 1907 to 1933. He led the local branch of the Polish Socialist Party. After spending four years in prison for revolutionary activities, he left with his family for France. On the Parisian street, Faubourg Saint-Jacques (not Saint-Jacques), he founded a photographic workshop, which soon became one of the best of its kind in the capital. He was the official photographer of Auguste Rodin's sculptures, and also photographed many French artists and politicians. In 1922 he made a portrait of Ilya Zdanevich. In 1933 he left for Poland, where he became an adviser to the government. He died in Łódź.

3 Mark Vladimirovich Talov (1892–1969) was Russian poet and translator, who was one of the founders of the Chamber of Poets [Палата поэтов] in Paris in 1921, a literary group of Russian émigrés. In 1922 he left for Berlin, and then for Soviet Russia.
　　Alexander Samsonovich Ginger (1897–1963) was a Russian poet and prose writer, a member of the the Chamber of Poets, and also the avant-garde leftist group, Through [Через].

He was a friend of the artist and writer Sergei Sharshun, as well as the poet Boris Poplavsky. He maintained friendly relations with Iliazd until his death.

4 'House on Shit: Intelligentsia and Empire', was a lecture Zdanevich gave in Paris in 1922.
　　Sergei Yuryevich Sudeikin (1882–1946) was a Russian painter who gained international fame for his set designs. Zdanevich knew him from St. Petersburg. In 1922, Zdanevich made calligraphic decorations (in the form of zaum verses) for the dress of the artist's wife V. Sudeikina.
　　After graduating from the Academy of Architecture in Vilnius, Jacques Lipchitz [Yakov Lipshits] (1891–1973), arrived in Paris in 1909, where he became a famous Cubist sculptor. In the 1920s he was close to the journal *Udar* and took part in the activities of the group Through and the Union of Russian Artists in Paris. In 1941, he fled from the Nazis to the United States.

5 A biography of the "naïve" poet Konstantin Gurgenov, who lived in Tbilisi and was the author of the book *Poems* published in Moscow in 1907, whose poems Iliazd cited from memory, remains practically unknown. The Futurist poet Yuri Marr considered him a "genius". The zaum poet Dimitry Gordeev, also from Tbilisi, was influenced by Gurgenov and planned a poetic

　　Iliazda at the Birthday Party

language for the "Middle-East Zaum International".

6 In fact, the name of the poet is Merkuriev. It was he who was the author of the poetic book *Demon: Eastern Novella by I.D. Merkuriev. His imitation of M. Lermontov*, published in Berlin in 1920.

7 "Sealed oak" – an expression from Terentiev's poem 'Travelling', published in his book *Fact* (1919). "Twirling imitation fetters" – a line from A. Kruchenykh's poem 'Merry Sacrifice' (1920), published in Весёлая жертва (1920).

8 "Wave and stone, verse and prose, ice and flame are not as different from each other" - a line from the second chapter of *Eugene Onegin*. "Neither day nor night, neither darkness nor light! .." – a line from part one of 'The Demon'.

9 Francis Picabia and Zdanevich were friends from 1922.

10 'Sunset over the Adriatic' was a painting exhibited in 1910 at the Salon des Indépendants under the assumed name of J. R. Boronali. In fact, it was created with the help of a donkey, to whose tail artists from Montmartre attached a brush with paint. This was done in order to mock the new abstract artist schools and critics.

11 M. Larionov called his group Donkey's Tail to express his rejection of elite art; the group's exhibitions also showed works by self-taught artists, children, etc.

12 *17 Nonsensical tools* [17 ерундовых орудий], a book by Igor Terentiev, published by 41 Degrees in 1919 in Tbilisi.

13 Viktor Ivanovich Bart (Victor Barthe, 1887–1954) was a Russian artist, a close friend of Ilya Zdanevich from St. Petersburg, and a classmate of his brother Kirill at the Higher Art School at the Imperial Academy of Arts in St. Petersburg. Participated in the second exhibitions of the Union of Youth (1911), as well as in the exhibitions 'Jack of Diamonds', and 'Donkey's Tail'. From 1916 he was in the Russian Expeditionary Corps in France. After the signing of a separate peace accord in 1918, he refused to participate in hostilities and was sent for hard labour in Algeria. Between 1919–1936 he lived in Paris, collaborated in the journal *Udar* [Strike], and joined the group Through.

14 The famous St. Petersburg beauty Salomea Nikolayevna Andronikova (1888–1982), sung about O. Mandelstam in the verse 'Straw' (1916) and A. Akhmatova in the verse 'Shadow' (1940), was an old friend of Zdanevich, who, when he lived in St. Petersburg, was passionately in love with her.

15 Sergei Matveyevich Romov (1883–1939) was a critic, art historian, publisher and translator. He had lived in Paris since 1906. He was a friend of the French Dadaists. He was a patron of young Russian poets and artists, and edited the Russian avant-garde journal *Udar*, published in Paris (1922–1923, four issues were published). In 1928, he went to the USSR, hoping to return soon to Paris, which he never succeeded in doing. After two arrests and accusations on political grounds, Romov was shot.

16 Ilya Zdanevich was born on 21st April 1894 in Tbilisi. In Paris, he usually celebrated his birthday on May 3rd.

17 Vasily Ivanovich Shukhaev (1887–1973) was a fellow student of Kirill Zdanevich at the Academy of Arts in St. Petersburg in 1911–1912, and later a member of the World of Art. The Shukhaevs, who settled in Paris in 1921, were Iliazd's closest friends.

18 Iliazd compares Merkuriev with the French self-taught artist Henri Rousseau (1844–1910), who served as a customs officer.

19 Perhaps this contains a playful allusion to Fatma Pesend Hanum (1876–1928), the eleventh wife of the Ottoman Sultan Abdul-Hamid II. She was known for leading a life of sadness, loneliness, and self-denial.

20 Konstantin Andreevich Tereshkovich (1902–1978) was one of the most famous Russian artists in Montparnasse; he was a member of the group Through. In 1920 he came from Baku via Constantinople to Paris, where he was especially close to Boris Poplavsky. In the 1920s and 1930s, while working for Coco Chanel, Iliazd helped Tereshkovich sell paintings to the company's clients and thus gained some fame among wealthy Parisians.

21 Young Ilya was indeed dressed as a girl, and called Ailey.

22 Igor Terentiev, *Tenderness Record: Life of Ilya Zdanevich* [41 Degrees, Tbilisi, 1919], translated by Pavel Smislajevs, forthcoming in *bie bao* series.

23 This theme is connected with the motif of the "shoe", which was voiced in the talk 'On Futurism'. In the report 'Worship of the Shoe', presenting himself as a shoe-shiner, Zdanevich said: "The earth is dirty... All mechanical culture, technical improvements and inventions are in the name of overcoming the boundaries set by the earth... The beauty of the body has died... replaced by the

Iliazda at the Birthday Party

recognition of beauty for the mechanical. It brings freedom from the earth and therefore it will conquer... To shine a shoe means to revive the knowledge of human freedom and the idea of freedom from the earth... It means to point out that the momentary triumph of the earth is in vain, the fallen one will rise and continue on an amazing path... a class of people has been created, dedicated to the revival of the shoe, and I am among them. The priests of a new religion came – a man liberated from the earth."

24 "Fetters", "hindrance", style of clothing that came into vogue in the 1920s: a feature of dresses or skirts in which the lower part of the dress or skirt is narrower than the top, which makes one walk in short steps.

25 After completing his studies at the university in the spring of 1917, the young lawyer Zdanevich compiled reports for the naval ministry of Alexander Kerensky and worked as an editor of the literary-political journal *Contemporary Papers* [Современные записки], published with the active participation of the Socialist Revolutionary Party from 1913 to 1917. Kerensky (1881-1970) was one of the leaders of the Socialist Revolutionary Party; after the February Revolution he worked in the ministries of Justice, and of War and the Navy; he led the Provisional Government ousted by the Bolsheviks with the October Revolution. From 1917 until his death he lived in exile.

26 Vladimir Mikhailovich Zenzinov (1880–1953) was a member of the Central Committee of the Socialist-Revolutionary Party, one of the writers for *Contemporary Papers*, the publisher of 'Narodnaya Gazeta', an active participant in the February Revolution and a member of the Executive Committee of the Petrograd Soviet. In 1919 he emigrated to France.

27 March 4th, 1917 in Petrograd, a meeting of artists chaired by Maxim Gorky formed a commission for the protection of monuments and the organisation of artistic affairs and put forward the idea of creation of the Ministry of Fine Arts. On March 7th, a commission was formed to draft the Ministry, chaired by Russian artist and art critic, the leader of the association 'World of Art' [Мир искусства] Alexander Nikolaevich Benois (1870–1960). In opposition to this initiative, on March 8th, an organisational meeting of the Federation of Leftist Artists and Writers titled 'Freedom to Art' was held and Ilya Zdanevich became the group's temporary secretary. In March they released an Appeal to the Artists. On March 12th, in the hall of the

Iliazda at the Birthday Party

Mikhailovsky Theatre, a city-wide rally of artists (more than 1,400 people) was held, where Zdanevich made a speech proclaiming the "separation of art from the state" and the demand to convene a Constituent Assembly of artists. After the debate, where he was supported by artist Nathan Altman, the director Vsevolod Meyerhold and the art theoretician Nikolay Punin, resolutions were adopted on the formation of the Union of Artists and on the convening of the Constituent Council. In the following days, Zdanevich actively participated in the creation of a broad coalition of left-wing forces for the freedom of art from the state tutelage. Together with the left, he entered the Union, but obviously, did not get onto its Council. On March 21st, speaking at the general meeting he faced the opposition of Mayakovsky, who declared his unwillingness to reckon with the Federation, but took a conciliatory position, offering the poet further negotiations. Mayakovsky's behaviour played an obvious role in the subsequent collapse of the Federation. Despite these splits, Zdanevich and the activities of the Federation prevented Benois from becoming the Minister of Culture.

28 Under the pen name Eli Eganbyuri, Zdanevich published a small book on Mikhail Larionov and Natalia Goncharova in 1913 .

29 An allusion to the avant-garde group Bloodless Murder (Бескро́вное убийство, 1915–1917) based in St. Petersburg, whose leaders were Mikhail Le Dentu and Olga Leshkova. The group edited a handwritten hectograph journal of the same name (1915–1916). In 1916, Zdanevich joined the group, writing his first zaum drama based on the special 'Albanian Edition' of the *Bloodless Murder* magazine.

30 Terentiev, *Tenderness Record.*

31 In the programme of the 'Dada lir kan' evening hosted by Sharshun on December 21st 1921, Zdanevich is presented as a "mezzo-soprano", which alludes to his high voice.

Sergei Ivanovich Sharshun (1888–1975) was an artist who left Russia for Paris in 1912. In 1920 he became close to a group of Dadaists (Tristian Tzara, Francis Picabia, and others). He participated in the Barres Trial, published a number of drawings and poems in Dadaist journals and in the activities of the group Through.

32 On the cover of A. Kruchenykh's *Lacquered Tights* [Лакированного трико, Tbilisi, 1919] there is a blurb for his book: "A trilogy from the life of the Mamudi [мамудийцев] people" with an explanation in brackets: "Khlebnikov - Mayakovsky - I. Zdanevich."

   Iliazda at the Birthday Party

33 "Take a poster and go to Yamudiya [Ямудию]!" – a phrase from the satirical work of M.E. Saltykov-Shchedrin *Pompadours and Pompadourshes* [Помпадуры и помпадурши] (1863–1874). In March 1918, in Tbilisi, Kruchenykh read the report 'Air Restaurant in Yamudiya'. In his book *Melancholia in a Robe* [Малохолия в капоте, Tbilisi, 1919] there is a section called the "History of Yamudiya", with citations from Saltykov-Shchedrin, Pushkin, Chekhov, D. Burlyuk, Mayakovsky, and others with phallic-vaginal connotations, including a word from Zdanevich's 'dra' *Yanko, King of Albania* – "mamudy".

34 Raymond Duncan (1874–1966) was an American painter and dancer, the elder brother of the dancer Isadora Duncan and creator of the Duncan Academy. He was friends with the Dadaists, although he did not share their views. He famously said about marriage: "Every marriage is a misalliance." Zdanevich connects his name with the name of F.T. Marinetti, who proclaimed a "contempt for women" in the name of fighting tradition.

35 'Poetry after Bath' was the title of a lecture by Zdanevich in Paris in 1922.

36 Citation from Mayakovsky's 'A Cloud in Trousers'.

37 An inaccurate citation from the verse 'To Everything'.

38 In October and November 1921, Khlebnikov lived in the North Caucasus, in Pyatigorsk, near Mount Mashuk. In the spring of 1922, the poet was already in very poor physical condition and died on June 28th. Ehrenburg spoke highly in 1921 about the poems of Vyacheslav Ivanov. In the next year, in the journal *Vešč'-Gegenstand-Objet,* he spoke about Khlebnikov like this: "I still expect him to formalise, realise his mission, and I believe that he will be Vyacheslav Ivanov of our days."

39 Blaise Cendrars (1887–1961) was a French-Swiss poet, writer, journalist, traveller and one of the greatest innovators in France. In 1908 he travelled around Russia. In collaboration with Sonya Delaunay he published thethe artist-book *Prose about the Trans-Siberian Express and Little Jehanne of France* in 1913.

40 Constantin Brancusi (1876–1957) was a Romanian sculptor and a regular in the Russian Cafés in Paris. The Café du Parnasse, founded in 1910, was located at 103 Boulevard Montparnasse. It housed a permanent exhibition of paintings by Cubist artists and the editorial office of art magazines.

41 *Veshch/Gegenstand/Objet: Mezhdunarodnoe obozrenie sovremennogo iskusstva / Internationale Rundschau der Kunst der Gegenwart / Revue internationale de l'art moderne*, was a a magazine edited by El Lissitzky and Ilya Ehrenburg in Berlin in 1922. Two issues were published.

42 Francis Jammes (1868–1938) was a French poet associated with Symbolism, especially with the poetics of Stéphane Mallarmé. In the 1920s–1930s he was one of the main opponents of the avant-garde and newer artistic movements. In the 1910s Ilya Ehrenburg translated the poetry of Francis Jammes.

43 This refers to Ilya Ehrenburg's book *Eves* (Кануны, Berlin, 1921).

44 Ehrenburg visited Tbilisi together with Osip Mandelstam in the autumn of 1920, which he recalled in his memoirs *People, Years, Life* (1960–1963).

45 In *Veshch/Gegenstand/ Objet* Ehrenburg stated: "True, you still have phenomena of Dadaistic measles (Kruchenykh, Zdanevich, Terentiev and some others). But they remain isolated cases, far from an epidemic. It is clear that our time requires a new language, but by no means "zaum", but "superintelligent", not a glossary of individual insanity, but synthetic words – terms of collective use."

46 Zdanevich received a passport as a citizen of the Democratic Republic of Georgia on May 26th, 1918, the day the new state was founded. He was Georgian by his mother and Polish by his father's side.

47 Kruchenykh: "... and here, among these outpourings of these faithful hearts, an ominous sound is heard – b r i!" From *Secret Vices Academicians* (Тайные пороки академиков, Moscow, 1916), together with Kazimir Malevich and Ivan Kliun.

48 Words used by F.M. Dostoyevsky in 'Winter Notes on Summer Impressions' (1863).

49 On the cover of Igor Terentiev's book on Zdanevich, *Tenderness Record*, designed by Zdanevich himself, a huge letter "yu (Ю)" is reproduced.

50 "Attempt with unsuitable means" is a legal term denoting an attempt to commit a crime with the help of such means and tools that objectively cannot cause the harm desired by the criminal (remember that Zdanevich was a lawyer by training). In the article dedicated to Boris Poplavsky, written shortly after the death of the poet (1935), Zdanevich calls himself and his fellow poets "the ideologists of poetry as 'an assassination attempt with unsuitable means'."

51 About the Russian obscene
alphabet, where each letter
was associated with an erotic
miniature, which was associated
with a no less obscene couplet.
The following verses belonged
to "Y": a letter that does not
begin words. The elephant
screams when he cums.

52 The State Duma met in the
Tauride Palace in Petrograd,
in February 1917. It housed the
Provisional Committee of the
State Duma, and then (until July
1917) the Provisional Government,
where Zdanevich served in the
Naval Ministry. It was here that
the Petrograd Soviet of Workers'
and Soldiers' Deputies arose.
Empty by February 1917, the
mansion of the famous ballerina
M. Kseshinskaya was turned
into the main headquarters of
the Bolsheviks. The Petrograd
Committee moved there, and
later the Central Committee of
the RSDLP (b).

53 Zdanevich heard Kerensky's
speech in the Tauride Palace on
March 2nd, 1917, about which the
politician wrote in his memoirs:
"I climbed onto the table and
began my speech. [...] I told
them that I, as the Minister of
Justice of the new government
considered it impossible to
wait longer for this step to be
approved by the Council."

54 This refers, probably, to one
of several speeches by V.I. Lenin
at the Finland Station, given
after his arrival in Petrograd
from exile on the night of April
3rd, 1917. In a letter to the
Federation of Soviet Writers'
Associations, written on June
24th, 1928, Zdanevich mentions
his presence at this historical
meeting of the leader of the
Bolsheviks.

55 Zdanevich left Petrograd
in May 1917 after he received
an invitation to participate in a
scientific expedition to North
Eastern Turkey under the
leadership of E.S. Takaishvili.

56 Lado Gudiashvili (1896–1980)
was an artist from Tbilisi, he had
been performing in Paris since
the beginning of 1920. In Paris,
where he became close to the
Dadaists, his paintings, which
foreshadowed Surrealism, soon
became a success. The exhibition
of his work, which Zdanevich
announced, was open from
May 26th to June 9th, 1922, and
showed forty-eight canvases.
Gudiashvili was a longtime friend
of Zdanevich and one of the
most zealous defenders of Niko
Pirosmani's work.

57 The first public performance
of Mayakovsky took place on
November 30th, 1912 in St.
Petersburg in the literary-
artistic cafe, Stray Dog.

Iliazda at the Birthday Party

58 Terentiev, *Tenderness Record*, forthcoming in *bie bao* series.

59 From July to September 1917, Zdanevich and Gudiashvili were part of an expedition organised by archaeologist E.S. Takaishvili on the former territories of North Eastern Turkey. Ishkhan is a village in this part of Turkey, where there is an ancient Orthodox church (from the first half of the 9th century), the copies of plans of which were made by Zdanevich.
In 1923, Zdanevich published his final 'dra', the play *lidantYU fAram*, dedicated to Mikhail Le Dentu.

60 Wilhelm von Wied (1876–1945) was a German Prince, who in 1914 became the puppet sovereign of Albania. He was one of the prototypes of Yanko from *Yanko, King of Albania*. The capital of Albania was then the city of Durazzo (Durres), hence the play on words used at that time "stupid view".

61 Cited from Zdanevich's 'dra' *Donkey for Rent* (1919).

62 Terentiev, *Tenderness Record*.

63 Ibid.

64 Ibid.

65 Ibid.

66 Jules Massenet (1842–1912) was a French composer and author of the lyrical dramas *Manon* and *Werther* which were very popular at that time. His works are a type of light and sentimental opera.

67 From Zdanevich's fourth 'dra', *Zga Yakaby* (1920).

68 Alexander Griboedov (1795-1829) was a Russian diplomat, poet, and composer who was also referred to by Khlebnikov and Kruchenykh.

69 This zaum verse is collected from six separate lines of the character "khazYain" [houst], scattered throughout the text of the drama *lidantYU fAram*.

70 The initial lines of *lidantYU fAram*, which was yet unpublished at the time of Zdanevich's lecture 'Iliazda'.
грАжани
вОйня наЯканая дЕтками Оли ляшкОвай АкалЕла вотАк ВзЯл
The literal translation would be: folks, the war-massacre proudly prophesied by the offspring of olga lyashkova has ingloriously-died, just like that [translator's note].

71 Terentiev, *Tenderness Record* (1919). In one of the illustrations by Kiril Zdanevich used in *Tenderness Record*, he depicted his brother as an angel flying on wings.

     Iliazda at the Birthday Party

72 In the flyer for subscribing
to *lidantYU fAram*, among
other opinions about himself,
Zdanevich cites S. Sudeikin's
statement that he was an "angel
millionaire." Here the words are
associated with the book of
poems by Kruchenykh, *Milliork*
(Tbilisi, 1919).

73 Serge Fotinsky (later
known as Abram Shulimovich
Aizensher, 1887–1971) was poet
and graphic artist, who lived
in Paris from 1908. He most
likely did not paint a portrait of
Zdanevich.

74 In 1913, N. Goncharova made
a graphic portrait of I. Zdanevich
with two wings.

Iliazda at the Birthday Party

50 Years of Russian Futurism

Iliazd – Ardengo Soffici
Correspondence

A Letter from Ardengo Soffici[1] to Iliazd

Poggio a Caiano
March 30th, 1963

Dear Sir,

I very much regret having been so busy speaking
with people who had arrived from Florence expressly
to see me, on that day that you came to Poggio in
order for us to chat.[2] When my wife gave me your
card and I saw who you were, I was eager to receive
you immediately, wanting so much to make your
acquaintance, but I knew you had already left. Alas!
My wife told me you would return, and your card gave
me reason to hope for as much. But that was quite
some time ago and I now have my doubts.

Our meeting would have been quite useful in
many regards, I feel. You could have brought me
news about Picasso, my old childhood friend Picasso,
of whom I have heard but rare and brief updates. You
could have told me about your book and the Futurist
movement and for my part I could have clarified
some things for your benefit, and shown you related
things and documents that would have perhaps
interested you and been of use to your work.

It was such a pity that this wonderful opportunity
slipped away.

Should you have written to me of some of the
things you would have said, I would have truly been
grateful: concerning Picasso, your work, how I could

be helpful to you. And very much so if you should
once again think of making the trip to Italy and
heading all the way to Florence and Poggio.
     My cordial salutations to you as I wait for you to
give me a sign.

     Yours truly,
     Ardengo Soffici

     A Letter from Ardengo Soffici to Iliazd

A Letter from Ardengo Soffici to Iliazd

Poggio a Caiano
December 29th, 1963

My Dear Friend,

I must thank you for your visit which gave me such
great pleasure. As may no doubt be clear to you, it
brought back to me the years of my youth in Paris, so
many of my friends, especially my dearest Picasso
whose regards you brought to me and gave me a
bracing joy.

It is too bad that your stay in Florence is so
short. If we had had a bit more time we could have
met again and discussed so many things that we
merely touched upon. In the hope of having you here
next year again as you promised, I am sending you
this with the request that you mention it to Picasso,
perhaps even showing him this letter. You could tell
him that three years ago, with the help of our mutual
friend Sabartès,[3] I tried to phone him at his home
near Cannes and give him my greetings, remind him
of our times together, and offer to see him if it would
be his pleasure to do so. Unfortunately we were
unable to communicate because of that disaster at
the time produced by a collapsing dike which flooded
the region. Last year I planned a similar trip but the
time I chose was not the best and I was not sure if
my visit would have suited Picasso. I now request
that you tell him these things, that you report the

memories that I have always maintained intact for
nearly half a century, and to ask him to let me know
(via yourself, if he cannot take the trouble to do it
directly) if I may have the pleasure next Spring of
greeting him in the area of the Midi where he will
be staying. This, so that I do not undertake the trip
otherwise, in vain.

I expect that you, dear friend, will keep your
promise to write to me, and I will keep my promise
to let you know if I manage to find something about
Marinetti at the Archivio di Stato.

Friendly wishes to you, and to your wife.
Ardengo Soffici

    A Letter from Ardengo Soffici to Iliazd

A Letter from Iliazd to Ardengo Soffici

50 Years of Russian Futurism

Dear Sir,
Dear friend,

I thank you for your invitation to come celebrate with
you the fiftieth anniversary of Russian Futurism. You
flatter me by saying that since it is I that introduced
Futurism to Russia in early 1912, that I cannot evade
my responsibilities. Believe me that I would love to
come to Florence and raise a glass on this occasion,
in that most backward-looking of cities. And to
reminisce about my early years at the dinner table,
relive for you the events of these fifty years. But
if I cannot come – and please forgive me for this
failure – it is not because I would have lacked ease
or liberty in my conduct. I refuse to be a narrator of
anecdotes. Writings on art have degenerated into an
odious slop of real or imagined stories, the books into
detestable collections of fake photos accompanied
by blathering. I do not want to keep them company.
The incurable and painful history of Russian Futurism
does not merit their approach.

We have come in order to solve problems in art
that were posed at the beginning of the century,
and not to solve crossword puzzles. We brought
modern art and modern poetry with us, and emerged
as victors everywhere. Except in Russia. This
failure poses the problem of ancillary art with an

extraordinary clarity, and it is this problem which makes of Russian Futurism a question still current today. No one addresses this, which is no surprise given the current situation of critical culture. Allow me thus to get your attention by asking that you forgive me for disappointing your expectations.

It is difficult to write in French about affairs that are Russian. Artistic life there has given rise to situations formerly unknown in France and terms which are lacking here. In order to translate them one must resort to encyclopaedic explanations as one does in exotic novels in which the author uses foreign terms in order to glean some local colour. It comes down to local colour in Russia as well, but one must reckon with it in order to understand the course of events.

The most important of these terms is *khaltura*.[4] Just as the word *intelligentsia*, the "class of intellectuals," has ended up penetrating journalistic speech in France, this term may also do the same, one day. It is used for an artwork that is superficial, shoddy, without any sincerity, and is close to the notion of commercial art. *Khaltura* is not necessarily a commercial painting or poem, but it is always a poor task that must be done. For example, the most recent history of official Russian painting is that of *khaltura*. But it is not rare to find *khaltura* in Russian abstract art either. What can always be said about it is that its being easily accepted by the client – it is never refused. In the early years of Futurism we devoted much time to the origin of this word.

    A Letter from Iliazd to Soffici

Several of the artists affirming difficult art would at the same time produce *khaltura* in order to get by. So it was, what one would call in the argot of libraries, *"drouille"* [crap]. Here in Paris I got to know some artists who, finding no outlet for their abstract art, would do drawings of people's heads that they would sell in the evenings at café terraces. They don't need that anymore and one day their drawings, hailed as figurative steps toward abstraction, will stand on a par with, or even be more valued than, their abstract art. We have already seen several such examples of their commercial use. *Khaltura* is related to the ancillary status of art. But it is not necessarily related to artistic impecuniousness. An artist from around here who, owing to the success of his work, received a good contract and increased the size and output of his work beyond measure, produces *khaltura* in the process of getting rich. His painting became the ancilla of commercial circulation. It is always a bad painting, but a bad painting is not always *khaltura.*

Since I will be obliged to discuss politics – and the first to begin mixing art with politics or, rather, aesthetics with politics was Marinetti himself – I will take the liberty to add to this letter a preliminary page making clear my position vis-à-vis the Soviet Union.

It is common knowledge that I never opposed it. Having never lived in Soviet territory, I have also been scrupulously loyal towards it. Indeed, I left Petrograd (now Leningrad) prior to October 1917 and Tiflis (now Tbilisi), my hometown, prior to February 1921.[5] I have never contributed to any migrants' publication, never

     A Letter from Iliazd to Soffici

taken part in the meetings of Russian writers here –
except for the few occasions I came to heckle – and
the Russian group *Tchérez* ("from above" or "across")
that we founded with passion together with Sergey
Romov had a pro-Soviet orientation. In 1925 I was
recognised by the government as a Soviet citizen,
and it was only administrative difficulties which
hindered my return. I even worked for the Soviet
embassy for two years as administrative assistant
to one of the secretaires.[6] Several publications
tried to slander me by writing that I was sent to
France by the Soviet government in 1920 in order
to organise an exhibition of Russian paintings. It's a
funny idea, but the author had to retract his story.
There was also the intrigue set up by two communist
poets following a newspaper article announcing
an upcoming production of my phonetic ballet *The
Undersea Chase* with set design by Henri Matisse
and with the participation of Yvette Chauviré and
Serge Lifar – incorrect information regarding the
latter – attacking me for associating myself with
Serge Lifar.[7] It would be interesting to find out what
reaction these malicious pedants, who were trying
to compromise me with false information, had when
the Soviet ambassador Mr. Vinogradov[8] appeared in
the newspapers in the company of Lifar, and when
Picasso did a sketch of him for his souvenir book.

My attitude is benevolent and free of prejudice
since I have never published in Russia and the
communist newspapers of Paris have never published
anything of mine either. If I am now proceeding to

   A Letter from Iliazd to Soffici

criticise the politics of the Russian communist party which has led to the disappearance of Futurism from the artistic scene, it is not to take up a position against the Soviet regime in a political sense. I will speak only of aesthetic matters and if I have gone on at length about my attitude towards the regime, it is so that no one can accuse me of hypocrisy and of using my historical overview of Russian Futurism as a screen for my attack on the Soviets.

I was born in Tbilisi in... Here I go, with a *curriculum vitae*, which is so much the fashion nowadays. All painting exhibitions are accompanied by the biography of the painter, obligingly displayed before the visitor with a brochure or a pamphlet. Prefaces, which had been the *sine qua non* of the heroic era, have become a rare thing. This is not surprising considering the vulgarity and poverty of criticism. But biographies, with their list of galleries and collections featuring the works of a painter, these have become compulsory. But have you noticed that this methodology coming from Germany via Switzerland is nothing other than a heritage of the Nazi era and its racial laws, when artistic or literary events required a *curriculum vitae*, especially if it were to start with the sentence: "*Ich bin Jude*"... Another country of *curriculum vitae* is the United States where they are deployed to track down communists. The other side of the same coin. The French art dealers seem not to be the initiators of this habit which has nothing to do with an artistic attitude. I don't need to delve into this story any further, but it is typical of the ancillary status of art which we shall discuss. I will thus leave out my age, my origins, and the position of my family. These things are only of interest for a police mind-set. On the other hand, it is important for the story of Futurism to mention that my father was a former Parisian and was a French professor after returning to his country. He used the school breaks to return there. And living in Paris was the dream of our youth, my brother and me. Artists who had lived in Paris were no rarity in my parents' entourage. One of them, the painter Boris Lopatinsky,[9] returning from Paris in 1911 where he had met F.T. Marinetti, brought back Marinetti's manifestos, Futurist paintings and books. For me, who had been an imitator of the Symbolists, this was a conversion.

I soon left for St. Petersburg (now Leningrad) in order to pursue my studies. There I met the Cubist painters Victor Barthe and Mikhail Le Dentu, who both introduced me to avant-garde artistic circles. The only thing I had on my mind then, was to spread the ideas of Futurism to those around me.

At the time, late 1911, Futurism's only exposure in Russia was a few short letters sent to the magazine *Apollon* by Paolo Buzzi.[10] The poet Mikhail Kuzmin[11] published an article mentioning the Futurism movement next to the letters in the same issue, but there were no Futurists in it. There were the Burliuk brothers, David and Nicolai; Aleksei Kruchenykh and painters like Mikhail Larionov and Natalia Goncharova who made up a group of young people, the Youth Union, in St. Petersburg, and who organised

   A Letter from Iliazd to Soffici

exhibitions and gatherings in St. Petersburg and Moscow. They were established as hostile to the Symbolists and to the artists in the constellation of magazines like *Mir Iskusstva* ("the world of art"), *Apollon*, *The Golden Fleece*, and *The Balance*.[12] It was effervescent, with new trends in a hurry to sweep away the official art of the *Peredvizhniki* as much as that of *Mir Iskusstva*. Obviously, some booklets were printed, some exhibitions mounted, but the principal weapon was the events, the public meetings where the audience could be harangued by speakers whose remarks excluded tolerance and whose framework was delimited by the expressions "long live..." and "down with..." In St. Petersburg we met at the Troitsky Theatre and the lecture hall of the Tenishev School, and in Moscow at the lecture hall of the Polytechnic Institute.

It was at the Troitsky Theatre, at an initiative of the Union of Youth, that I made my declaration of January 18th, 1912 (in Julian calendar) fifty years ago.[13] The next day all groups, scenes, and youth groups became Futurists.

Up to then a buzzword was missing, one that could unite everyone in opposition to the art of the day. All I did was offer this word: Futurism.

With incredible speed this foreign word acquired all its meanings in Russia. If *Mir Iskusstva,* edited by Alexander Benois, had been a scene of aesthetes only known to specialists, Futurism by contrast became truly popular. Adopting the approach of the *Peredvizhniki* [The Wanderers][14] who took their name

     A Letter from Iliazd to Soffici

from their way of touring Russian cities with their
exhibitions, the Futurists became wanderers with
their events that a clever booking agent would set
up in one city after the next, making it a household
name. And Futurism became *futura*. I will not say
that the core of Russian Futurism was an ignorance
of Italian Futurism, or that it played the role of the
sorcerer's apprentice, but it is true that Russian
Futurism cared little about being in line with Italian
Futurism. From the start, it wasn't the same doctrine.
Italian Futurism came from the evolution of F.T.
Marinetti and his friends. Russian Futurism was the
application of words in freedom which was a vaguely
similar trend that began earlier. Each school laid
claim to being the true Futurism. We came to see the
Ego-Futurists, the Cubo-Futurists, the *boudetlianié*
(Russian translation of the word "Futurist" by
Khlebnikov). And the Italian Futurists ended up
being called the Italo-Futurists [italo-futuristes].
Mayakovsky and Pasternak were from different
categories of Futurists.

Such was the tendency to call all new art
"Futurist" that even artistic movements that no one
here would associate with Futurism, such as Cubism
or Fauvism, were included under its banner. Only later,
when the initial enthusiasm had waned, did particular
labels reappear, such as Constructivism, etc.

What did Russian Futurism augur? War or
revolution? Or one and the other. With fifty years'
hindsight it seems more profoundly Russian despite
its foreign name and facade, more so than many

movements with decidedly Russian façades. Stop
and look at this group of the Wanderer Painters,
the *Peredvizhniki*, that pass themselves off as being
thoroughly Russian painting. The taste one finds in
these paintings, its palette, its realism, are purely
German, and its theories are always very pro-
German and anti-French (Stasov).[15] Don't forget
this movement, the Wanderers. Keep an eye on this
monster at all times, these spinners of tales that are
falsely populist, and you will then better understand
the source of the portraits of Stalin's generals shown
at the Paris International Exposition of 1936, just
prior to the last war, as well as all the official Russian
art of the last thirty years. These are German works!
All the while having been and still being anti-German
politically, Russia never ceases to practice art of
German origins, to cultivate German taste. This
contradiction under its different forms appears to
us all along our account and forms the framework of
ancillary art.

Do not ask me what differentiates Russian
Futurism from Italian Futurism. Ask rather what
makes them similar. Not their politics. F.T. Marinetti's
patriotism, his battle of Tripoli and Balkan war
prior to it, are all quite foreign to Russian Futurists.
Their battles are against the past, against that
great Russian literature, against that great Russian
language. These were its real battles. To put it
bluntly, what interested the Russians in Marinetti's
actions and the Futurist painters were only the
events prior to 1912, that's where they drew their

    A Letter from Iliazd to Soffici

strength, as if the subsequent activity of the Italians escaped their notice. The package of manifestos and catalogues that I brought to St. Petersburg at the end of 1911 was and remained to be the field of contact between the Russians and the Italians.

F.T. Marinetti came to Russia at the beginning of 1914. It is remarkable that this trip is so absent within the archive of Futurism. We have no single document, no letter of his that gives evidence of this trip or confides in us his impressions during his stays in St. Petersburg and Moscow. We only know that he effectively went to and returned from Russia from the letters written by his friends.

This poverty of information has helped certain historians of modern painting affirm that F.T. Marinetti went to Russia several times, the first time in 1911 even. I cannot say if Marinetti went to Russia before 1910, but he surely did not between the years 1910 and 1914.[16] The assertion that he went there before 1911 in order to see what the Russians were doing and to use their approaches in Italy, an opinion formulated by Mikhail Larionov, is merely scaffolding aimed to establish a Russian antecedence in the invention of Futurism.

Did he foresee the upcoming war and did he have intentions other than to get to know the Russian Futurists? I don't know. But there are certain odd aspects about his stay – especially his silence after this trip.

True, it was not a success. During that week in Moscow I was there at his conference at the Society

     A Letter from Iliazd to Soffici

of Free Aesthetics.[17] We had hoped he would let loose against old Russia and call for the destruction of the Kremlin. But like any polite foreigner, he only thundered against Rodin! On that day he may well have saved the Kremlin.

There were protests by Futurists who were asked to answer in French, and a meeting the following day to issue an anti-Marinetti manifesto affirming there was nothing in common between the Russian and Italian Futurists. I refused to sign it. I only saw Marinetti again ten years later in Paris.

The commotion set off by Marinetti's arrival, which also served to increase animosity among the Russians, neither ended nor subsided when the war broke out.

Marinetti was right: the only hygiene the world knows is war. Without this miserable war, from one state Duma to the next we would have never been rid of the Tsarist regime.

By the eve of the jolt of February 1917 the activity of the Futurists who had been swept aside by the war started to reawaken with a new angle: no more manifestos. Theories and discoveries now took on plastic features.

I abandoned words set free, such as in the poem *Roland Garros*, in order to only pursue transmental poetry (*zaum*.) Together with Olga Leshkova, Nikolay Lapshin, Mikail Le Dentu, we started issuing the hectographed newspaper *Bloodless Murder*. I wrote the play *Yanko, King of Albania* which only saw publication two years later because the military

censors had seen in it a satirical representation
of the Tsar. But the play was performed in 1916, in
Stéphanie Essen's workshop, with set and costumes
by Mikhail Le Dentu and music by Mikhail Kuzmin.

With the advent of Lettrism, there was much talk
about my being the source of the creation of the *zaum*
language. Allow me to clearly explain my position.

The word *zaum*, "on the other side of
intelligence" – the closest translation because the
French expression "an intelligent man" corresponds
exactly to the Russian *um-nyi* and that for the
expression "on the other side of reason" one
would have required the Russian word *razum*, the
translation "transmental," as I first translated it, is
more inexact because "mental" corresponds to the
Russian *myslennyi* – is not mine, but was introduced
by Khlebnikov. I avoided using this term and for my
Yanko, as is mentioned in the prologue, the writing
is in "Albanian." Khlebnikov never made up phonetic
words completely abstracted from meaning, in
the layman's sense, so to speak. All of his writing
beginning with *Smekhatchi*, published in 1911, are
assembled from words produced by a play on root
words transfigured by a special use of prefixes and
suffixes.[18] The meaning of the word strays from
intellect, from consonance, and becomes imprecise
to reason, but immediate for emotion, producing
charm or bewitchment.

Kruchenykh created phonemes – for instance
his celebrated *dyr bul shchyl* – encrusted in layman's
terms, the way that Antonin Artaud did so in

     A Letter from Iliazd to Soffici

France, whereas I, for my part, created a phonetic
language acting on emotions through sonority and
associations with everyday language, much farther
from meaning than is the case with the words of
Khlebnikov. I wrote orchestral poetry for several
voices simultaneously that could be performed
on stage, and choreographic poetry in which the
accompanying dance is directed, without music,
by the syllables. *Estr Eyland* was one such dance,
presented at the Paris gallery *La Boétie* in 1923,
performed by Lizica Codreanu-Fontenoy, as well as
the the ballet I wrote in 1947, *The Undersea Chase*,
that I organised with Yvette Chauviré, and that was
sabotaged, as I have mentioned to you above. In
this later period I began using the term "poetry of
unknown words"[19] which thereby included all forms
of poetry that we now call phonetic or abstract.
For if we, the Russian Futurists, were the first in
this approach, when all is said and done, we were
certainly soon not alone.

I only began using the term *zaum* in 1919 in Tbilisi,
after the founding of the University of the 41 Degree
with Aleksei Kruchenykh and Igor Terentiev, and used
it to qualify our creations, mine in particular.

The day of the Revolution of February 22nd [8
March in Gregorian calendar] I had stopped by the
Duma, where I had a job in a legal commission, having
received my law degree a few weeks earlier. I had
turned down all the official positions I was offered
at the time. I was busy at the Academy of Fine Arts
and at public gatherings, waging my war against the

     A Letter from Iliazd to Soffici

plan to found a Ministry of Fine Art, a project set in motion by the *Mir Iskusstva* circle who wanted Sergei Diaghilev to come back from abroad to be offered the post of minister. But in the month of May, with my degree in hand, I decided to go see my parents and left Petrograd, never to return, alas.

At that moment I made a mistake that changed my life. In order to satisfy the wishes of a professor friend of my father's, and to continue pursuing childhood dreams, when we spent our Lents and vacations in the ruins of old convents, I took part in an archeological mission to Turkey. I, the first Russian Futurist. This is the episode that I have dragged like a ball and chain throughout my life, that has made me waste so many years and embark upon such a long and fruitless undertaking only to arrive at the conviction, so many years after Agrippa, that erudition is vain and poetry is perennial.

I returned from Turkey after the October Revolution. A barrier of red and white republics and of civil war was going up between Moscow and me. With my law school degree I went into a printing press as an apprentice typographer. This allowed me to compose and print *Yanko, King of Albania*, my first book. Soon afterwards, together with Kruchenykh and Terentiev, I started publishing and the University of the 41 Degree. Kruchenykh had already published several of his books in Moscow and Petrograd. But Terentiev, that remarkable youngster of Futurism, began under my care with *17 Nonsense Instruments*, the seventeen instruments of creative work.

 A Letter from Iliazd to Soffici

In order to explain the mediocrity of poetic work nowadays, references are made to there being no freedom of expression, to the ancillary state of art, basically, of poetry over there. If this state of affairs prevents new forces from finding expression, it nonetheless also plays no role in the *inexpressionism* of the entire poetic vocabulary. Because after us all words became dead. Sealed. Poets no longer have the power to resurrect them.

Marinetti did not take up Mussolini's ideas from the very start, but little by little as Fascism began to crystallise, Marinetti was on the way to becoming a luminary of the Fascist state. I do not know to which extent Futurism was popular in Italy. Was it but the privilege of a small group, a movement for artists, a poetry for poets, as is common today? Did it penetrate the masses, acquire a popularity like in Russia where, ultimately with Mayakovsky, it became the official art? I don't know. I haven't lived in Italy and the war prevented me from following the development of Italian poetic thought. When, much later, while editing *Poésie des Mots Inconnus* in 1948, I began to search for examples of such poetry, I could not find any. Aldo Palazzeschi, perhaps?[20] But where and when? While German poetry reached abstraction with Hugo Ball, Raoul Hausmann, and Kurt Schwitters, and French poetry with Hans Arp, Nicolas Beauduin, Paul Dermée, Pierre Albert-Birot, Vicente Huidobro, all under the banner of Dada, Italian Futurism did not manage to do so, having become didactic after the war due to its confusion

  A Letter from Iliazd to Soffici

with Fascism. D'Annunzio's adventure played out
in Trieste was but plagiarism of Marinetti's idea.[21]
Marinetti was not even an éminence grise. (Paolo
Buzzi wrote in *Apollon* that the young Futurists
admired D'Annunzio. Was it not the recurrence
of this admiration that prevented Marinetti from
taking action, despite his formula "the gods depart,
D'Annunzio remains"?)

It would be hard to find in history examples
of such ruination of a poetic idea. Marinetti let it
happen. He withdrew. One can regret it from the
perspective of historical clarity. Marinetti in Trieste,
one can't know if the undertaking would have been a
greater success than D'Annunzio's, but it would have
certainly not turned Marinetti into an academician, a
facet of the regime, a henchman that death in Milan
saved from the humiliation of the parades of the
American boots. By giving D'Annunzio a free hand,
the Futurist Marinetti did not only deal the death
blow to Italian Futurism, he did the same to Russian
Futurism. I created you and I will annihilate you.

I did not see Marinetti after his Moscow date
until 1923, in Paris, where he was passing through
again and introduced me to his young wife, while
stressing that it was but a civil union. I remember
nothing of our discussions then. I would only see him
again in 1937 at the Père Lachaise cemetery for the
anniversary of Apollinaire's death.

Mayakovsky met Apollinaire in Paris in 1925. He
would later write that he was surprised at himself for
having shaken hands with Marinetti, that Fascist. In

    A Letter from Iliazd to Soffici

1937, during the Spanish Civil War Picasso refused to shake hands with him. These little incidents mark out in fact a great drama.

In communist Russia the word Futurism would necessarily have to disappear from common use. As early as 1925 the slogan and the directive for the painters was: "without *futura*." The theories and directives that replaced Futurist art with *art pompier* would come later.

It will soon be forty years since Futurism departed from the Soviet context. But Futurism is not dead. Its role, so to speak, has not ended. Has it become clandestine? I don't know. But the inability of the regime to create a Soviet art, a Soviet poetry, a great art that is up to the great cause, means that everything meriting attention remains nothing more than the reflection of Russian Futurism, that decidedly does not wish to die. The imitators of Mayakovsky, Pasternak and Zabolotski,[22] who owed so much to Khlebnikov, were or are nourished by the sap of Futurism. Scratch the Soviet writer and you will find the Futurist writer. But we have never seen a fiasco such as the one following the application of Zhdanov's theories.

One of the most important actions for the defence of modern art was Picasso's joining the communist party.[23]

Imagine the situation of avant-garde art if he had not joined, if Picasso had stayed in the same apolitical position, with the excuse that one cannot take sides openly or tacitly, as many renowned

     A Letter from Iliazd to Soffici

artists say today? If communist painting had only been Soviet painting and in France André Fougeron,[24] and a few other neo-*pompiers*?

To attenuate the extraordinary effect that Picasso's painting be the painting of a communist, a multitude of diversions have been undertaken in different directions.

The Lenin Prize given to Picasso honours him as a humanist, the artist of Guernica, of the Korean War, his thought persistently aimed towards peace. It deviates the attention from his art towards humanitarian thinking. In France the communist press deliberately disguises his art by focusing on his works that are the least inventive, least dangerous, pictorially the most harmless. And then come the accusations from certain critics against his work, that he is duplicitous: one line of production for the communists, another for the perverse bourgeoisie. Please note that the authors of these accusations preferred the pictorially harmless Picasso, and find that any inventive action undertaken by a painter is nothing other than flattering of the jaded, perverse tastes of the bourgeoisie and their *je ne sais quoi*.[25]

Because of their tendency to smooth out Picasso's work, those French communists loyal to the unfortunate directives that come from the party in Moscow are themselves completely liable.

Picasso is too big to fight with openly. One tries as much as possible to diminish the glaring contradiction between his work and the party's artistic doctrine.

A Letter from Iliazd to Soffici

It is in this striking contradiction that resides
the no less striking historical merit of Picasso. Faced
with Russian *art pompier,* he declares that one can
be a communist, a so-very-active communist – not
a salon communist of which there are so very many
throughout the world – and also be a free painter. His
joining the communist party will make possible the
return of Futurist tendencies in Russia, and the end
of the dark Stalinist era which ends on the political
level continues to be extraordinarily healthy on the
artistic and literary level. The episode of the Stalin
portrait is worth mentioning here.[26]

I am not a slave. I am not a bureaucrat and I am
not obliged to know what one should and what one
shouldn't do. I am a poet. And if there are efforts
today to again try to reduce poets to the status of
lackeys that they had in the past, after the liberation
that Romanticism brought them, I write exactly in
order to describe the reasons for this change.

    A Letter from Iliazd to Soffici

1 Ardengo Soffici (1879–1964),
was an Italian artist, writer,
and poet. He joined Futurists
in 1913. In the 1920s and 1930s
he supported traditional
art and Fascism. Because
of his support for Mussolini
and active engagement with
Fascist institutions, he was
put in prison for a few months
following the Second World
War. Soffici wrote to Iliazd in
1963 asking him to take part in a
meeting with Italian specialists
where he would talk about the
emergence of Russian Futurism.
Zdanevich's letter is a response
to this inquiry.

2 In March 1963, Zdanevich
went to Arcetri, near Florence,
for "professional" reasons
to edit the notebooks of
astronomical observations
taken by Ernst Guillaume
Tempel (1821–1889), who had
worked at the observatory of
Arcetri. Tempel's personality
had attracted Zdanevich by
its originality because, during
his lifetime, this astronomer
without any degree or certificate
of study in astronomy had
suffered the disdain of
many of his colleagues who
refused to recognise his
discoveries, among which was
a star that Tempel had named
'Maximiliana'.

3 Jaime Sabartès (1881–1968),
was a Catalan Spanish artist,
poet and writer. He was a close
friend of Pablo Picasso and later

became his secretary. In the
1960s he initiated the founding
of the Picasso Museum in
Barcelona.

4 *Khaltura* is one of the Russian
words that became popular
after the October Revolution.
It can mean fraudulence,
charlatanism, a job done badly,
commercial art or kitsch. In
1922 Zdanevich gave a lecture
titled 'Berlin and its Khaltura',
forthcoming in the *bie bao
series* in a translation by Jyrki
Siukonen.

5 In February 1921 the
Russian Red Army occupied
the Democratic Republic of
Georgia aiming to overthrow the
Social-Democratic (Menshevik)
government and to install a
Bolshevik regime in the country.

6 Zdanevich actually worked
as a translator in the Soviet
Embassy in France for a few
months between 1924 and 1926.
There he was introduced to two
Georgian Bolshevik friends, one
of whom, Levan Gogoberidze,
became the First Secretary
of the Communist Party of
Georgia; the other, Nikolai
Piroumov, was convicted of
spying and expelled from France
in 1925. Both were executed
in Stalin's purges in 1937.
Zdanevich, never himself a Party
member, was during these years
a "fellow traveller".

     A Letter from Iliazd to Soffici

7 An unrealised drama that Zdanevich hoped to perform in the 1940s in the style of his old *dras*. Zdanevich hoped Henri Matisse would do the set design. Yvette Chauviré (1917–2016) was a French prima ballerina and actress. Serge Lifar (1905–1986) was a Ukrainian ballet dancer and choreographer. Lifar was politically right-wing and was a collaborationist in occupied France during the Second World War.

8 Sergey Vinogradov (1907–1970) was a Russian diplomat and the USSR ambassador to France from 1953 to 1965.

9 Boris Lopatinsky (1881–1946) was a painter, graphic artist, and publisher. He lived in Tbilisi in the early 1910s, where he was involved in avant-garde groups with Zdanevich.

10 Paolo Buzzi (1874–1956) was an Italian Futurist playwright and poet. Extracts from *The Manifesto of Futurist Painters* was translated into Russian in Buzzi's article 'Letters from Italy', which appeared in the *Apollon* journal in St. Petersburg in 1910.

11 Mikhail Kuzmin (1872–1936) was a Russian poet, musician and novelist. He was associated with Symbolist and Akhmeist schools.

12 Мир искусства (1898–1904), Золотое руно (1906–1910), Аполло́н (1909–1917), and Весы́ (1904–1909), were Russian language art magazines mostly with Symbolist tendencies.

13 The Union of Youth [Союз молодёжи] was a Russian artistic association that existed from 1909 to 1917 in St. Petersburg. The association did not have a definite programme, but instead its members and the sponsors of its exhibitions adhered to various artistic trends, including Symbolism, Cézannism, Cubism, Futurism, and abstract art.

14 Peredvizhniki was a name for the Russian realist painters from the second half of the 19th century. Ilya Repin was their most known representative.

15 Vladimir Stasov (1824–1906) was a very influential Russian art critic from a noble family.

16 Kjeld Bjørnager Jensen assures this in his article 'Marinetti in Russia, 1910, 1912, 1913, 1914?', published in *Scando-Slavica.15:1* in 1969 and concludes that "One can thus assume that Marinetti was not in Russia in 1910, and that the visit in 1914 was probably his first."

17 The Society of Free Aesthetics (Общество свободной эстетики) was active from 1906 to 1917 in

 A Letter from Iliazd to Soffici

Moscow. The society supported all tendencies within modern art. In February 1914, they organised a lecture by Marinetti in Moscow, followed by a discussion with Zdanevich.

18 Most probably Zdanevich is referring to Velimir Khlebikov's poem 'Incantation by Laughter' [Zaklyatie Smekhom], published in 1910, which is a derivational poem based on permutations built on the root *smekh* ("laughter").

19 *Poésie des mots inconnus* [Poetry of Unknown Words] is an artist book Iliazd published in 1949 in Paris in his 41° editions. Lavishly designed by Iliazd himself, this precursor of artist-books included poems by Albert-Birot, Arp, Artaud, Khlebnikov, Kruchenykh, Schwitters, Seuphor, Terentiev, Tzara, and many others. The volume was illustrated by Braque, Chagall, Dominguez, Giacometti, Gleizes, Hausmann, Léger, Matisse, Miró, Picasso, Taeuber-Arp, and others.

20 Aldo Palazzeschi (1885–1974) was an Italian novelist associated with Futurists in the 1910s. He fell out with Marinetti because of the Futurists open alliance with Fascism. He re-emerged as an experimental writer after the Second World War.

21 Gabriele D'Annunzio (1863–1938) was an Italian poet and ultra-nationalist, involved in extreme right-wing militarism. He was an influence on Marinetti.

22 Nikolay Zabolotsky (1903–1958) was a Soviet poet and translator. He was one of the founders of the Russian avant-garde absurdist group *Oberiu*.

23 "My joining of the Communist Party is the logical outcome of my whole life, of all my work." Pablo Picasso, 'Why I Became a Communis [1944]', *Picasso's Guernica*, edited by Ellen C. Oppler, W. W. Norton, New York, 1988, p. 251.

24 André Fougeron (1913–1998), was a French realist painter dealing with political subjects. After the Second World War, Fougeron became the official painter of the French Communist Party.

25 A quality that cannot be described or named easily.

26 Picasso drew a portrait of Stalin which appeared on the cover of *Les Lettres Francaises* on March 12th 1953, a week after Stalin's death.

A Letter from Iliazd to Soffici

Homage to IZ

Johanna Drucker

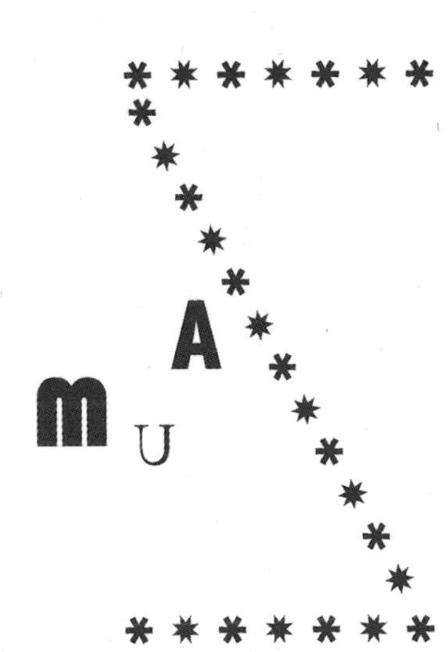

1 flea
2 donkey
3 cretin
4 angel
5 poet
6 dancer
m
A
u

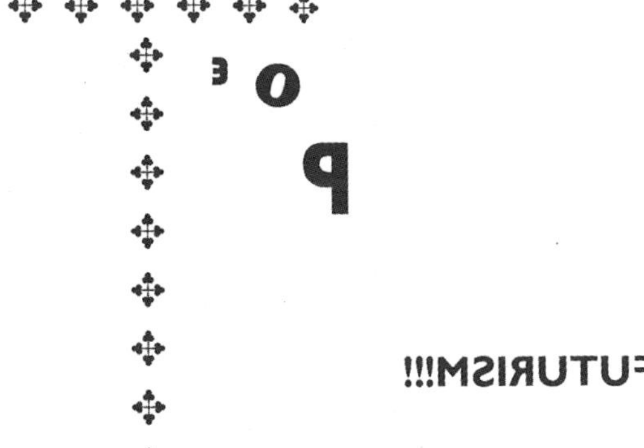

p
o
e
FUTURISM!!!

1	Avant-garde	Orthography	Art of the book
2	Poetic language	Constellations	Exquisite typography
3	Grammar	Rigorous works	Symmetrical designer
4	Poetry in grains	Modest labors	Pleated vellum
5	Transmental verse	Research	Plates etched in acid
6	Composition	Transparent	Companions

1	Illusion	Wandering Frair	Lettrist battles
2	Zaum dramas	Poems and blocks	Flags raised as signs
3	Ballet submarine	Unknown words	Letters made of wood
4	Dance of the North	Writing in reverse	Church Plans
5	Skinnybones	Horses at midnight	Study of astronomy
6	Just a hint	Travels in Africa	Selling a telescope

1	Young cadet	Exhibition	Primitivism
2	St. Petersburg	Larionov	Forty-one Degrees
3	Cabaret Fantastique	Goncharova	Rayonism
4	Constantinople	Ledentu, Kyril	Everythingism
5	Paris, Rue Mazarine	Pirosmani	Easter Eyeland
6	Trigance mountains	Marinetti	King of the Albanians

A Life iN LeTtErs & PageS

SO YOUNG SPEAKING TO THE DONKEYS POSING
AS A LOVER, SUITOR. SITTING ON A THRONE IN
THE GUISE OF A FLEA. THE POET ASPIRES TO RAD-
ICAL EFFECTS. TRANSFORMATION OCCURS IN
THE MAGIC OF ZAUM IN THE TONGUE, CHEEK,
MOUTH OF THE WRITER TURNING THE PEARLS
OF LANGUAGE INTO VERSE. A FERVOR IN THE FUTUR-
IST MOMENT, UPHEAVAL AND EXCITEMENT IN
THE AFFRONT TO PUBLIC TASTE. GROUPS FORMED
QUICKLY AND DISSOLVED AFTER RHETORICAL
FERVOR. PASSION RISES THE DISCOVERY OF A
GEORGIAN PAINTER, PRIMITIVE AND AUTHENTIC,
R THROUGH THE DAYS OF WAR AND REVOLU-
TION, COLLECTIONS MADE AND PEAKS
CLIMBED. THE YEARS SHIFT GEARS AND
MOUNTAINS PROVIDE REFUGE AS WELL
AS SITES OF ARCHAEOLOGICAL EXPEDI-
TIONS. INTRIGUED BY THE SYMMETRY OF
ORTHODOX CHURCHES, THEIR PLANS A
TEMPLATE FOR BOOK DESIGN LATER
PERFECTION BALANCED EXACTLY.
ORDEALS OF TRAVEL, DESTINATION
PARIS THE DIFFICULTIES OF REALI-
TY, SLEEPING ON FLOORS, A DEATH
SHIP, REFUGEES AND THE EFFECTS
OF WAR. FLOATING ON THE
BLACK SEA. CONSTANTINO-
PLE AND STUNNING BEAU-
TY OF THE HAGIA SOFIA
THE CONSTANT EDGE OF
HUNGER, WRITING. PARIS AT

LAST, THE VIBRANT SCENE AN INTERNATION-
AL COMMUNITY. RUSSIAN BALLS, COLLEAGUES,
CONNECTIONS, FINAL ZAUM SET AT THE PRINT
SHOP STANDING AT THE CASE, HOURS WITH
THE STICK IN HAND TO JUSTIFY THE COMPLEX
FORMS. LEDENTU, THE MASTERWORK, FALLS
INTO HISTORICAL GAPS AND SINKS, BEAUTIFUL,
UNIQUE, UNREADABLE, A HISTORICAL ANOM-
ALY OUT OF SYNCH. NECESSITIES ARISE, LOVE,
FAMILY, TASKS, AND EMPLOYMENT THE TEXTILE
INDUSTRY, FOR CHANEL UP TO THE MOMENT.
THE WAR, DIVORCE, THE CHILDREN, TURN EV-
ERYTHING AWAY. WRITING AND PRINTING, OP-
TIMISM OF RETURN TO DESIGN PRODUC-
TION, CRASHED WITH THE OUTBREAK
OF CONFLICT. SURVIVE. NEW LOVE, NI-
GERIAN, A PRINCESS DEAD TOO SOON
ALMOST IMMEDIATELY, TUBERCULOSIS,
LEFT A CHILD. THE BOOKS BEGIN AGAIN,
A CONFLICT WITH THE LETTRISTS,
SPARKS A MAJOR ANTHOLOGY OF
MODERN EXPERIMENTAL VERSE,
THE POETRY OF UNKNOWN
WORDS, SO IMPORTANT, COM-
PLEX, SO REPLETE. THE WHO'S
WHO OF THE EARLY 20TH
CENTURY EXPERIMENTAL
AVANT-GARDE. THE UN-
BOUND PAGES, PLEATED
VELLUM OF THE COVER,
WARNING NOT TO CUT

FROM

THE BEGINNING
TO THE END

LETTERS

CONSTELLATE

LIKE

STARS

2022, rekcurD annahoJ, ZI ot egamoH

THE EDGES, AN ACHIEVEMENT LIKE NO OTHER LEADS TO
THE NEXT AND NEXT A QUARTER OF A CENTURY WITH
ONE EDITION FOLLOWING ANOTHER. EVERY BOOK
BALANCED TO THE LETTER, SYMMETRICAL TO AN
OBSESSIVE EXTREME THAT REGISTERS AS PERFEC-
TION TO THE EYE. THE TONE AND TEMPER OF THE
WORKS ALWAYS ELEGANT AND ADVENTUROUS,
FOCUSED ON THEMES DANCE, EXPLORATION,
LANGUAGE. SOME PERSIST ACROSS THE LIFE,
ZAUM AND PIROSMANI, LEDENTU AND THE
MOUNTAINS, DEDICATION TO POETIC IN-
VENTION THROUGHOUT. AT THE END, A
RETURN THROUGH REWORKING THE
LINES, THE BOUSTROPHEDON RE-
VISITS LIFE FROM FINISH TO BEGIN-
NING THROUGH REVERSE, RIGHT
READING AND LEFT TO TURN
THE PROSE OF EXISTENCE
INTO POETRY. A LIFE, LIVED
IN LANGUAGE, WROUGHT
IN FINELY PERFECT FORM
ON THE PAGE. ILIAZD,
THE POET, THE DESIGN-
ER, THE DANCER, THE
SCHOLAR, LEFT THE
RECORD OF HIS LIFE
PRINTEDCHO-
REOGRAPHED
TYPOGRAPHIC
SCORED WORK
ALL SPEAKING
VOLUMES.